The
Peaceful
Way

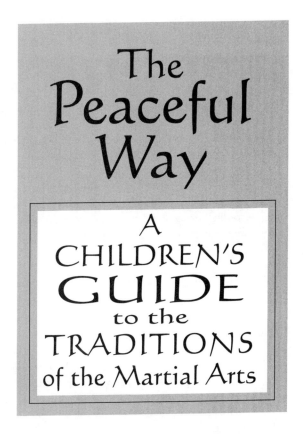

The Peaceful Way

A CHILDREN'S GUIDE to the TRADITIONS of the Martial Arts

Claudio Iedwab
and Roxanne Standefer

Illustrations by Claudio Iedwab

Destiny Books
Rochester, Vermont

Destiny Books
One Park Street
Rochester, Vermont 05767
www.InnerTraditions.com

Destiny Books is a division of Inner Traditions International

Library of Congress Cataloging-in-Publication Data
Iedwab, Claudio A.
    The peaceful way : a children's guide to the traditions of the
martial arts / Claudio Iedwab and Roxanne Standefer.
        p. cm.
    Summary: Explains the study and teaching of the martial arts,
emphasizing the philosophical aspects of this sport.
    ISBN 0-89281-929-4
    1. Martial arts—Juvenile literature. [1. Martial arts.]   I.
Standefer, Roxanne L. II. Title.
    GV1101.35 .J43 2001
    796.8—dc21
                                                2001002778

Printed and bound in Canada

10 9 8 7 6 5 4 3 2 1

Text design and layout by Kristin Camp
This book was typeset in Stempel Schneidler with Calligraphic as the
display typeface

To all those who participate in the global dojo of askSensei.com.

Contents

Acknowledgments

We are grateful for the inspiration of the young people of GORINDO "the Friendly Martial Art," particularly Hamish, Kim, Taylor, Trevor, Gillian, Scott, Ross, and Daniel, whom we kept in mind when we wrote this book.

We also deeply appreciate the help of our neighbors Elson, Joan and Bill, John "the tree sensei," Tom and Laura at L'Amable Variety, Industry Canada for CAP, Richard of The Great Escape, Roy "the UPS guy," Vaughn sensei, and the family Lord.

We would like to thank Rosemary Morrison and Raymond Standefer for not letting us starve and Bernardo and Linda Iedwab for an apple a day.

Claudio fondly remembers his early teachers Hipólito Elías sensei, Norberto "Toto" Moscovich, and Manuel Nieves Cao sensei for treating him like a human being, not "a kid." Also Samanta and Esteban, who many years ago at a very early age provided him with the first stepping stones for teaching young students.

Introduction

Welcome to the world of the martial arts. You are entering a special tradition that has a long history. Here you will find mysteries, feats of superhuman strength, wise teachers, and energetic students like yourself.

Discover the many stories and different paths to follow through the forest. If you are lucky enough to have a teacher in the martial arts, he or she will share new and exciting knowledge with you. You are going to have a lot of fun if you listen carefully and are ready to train with all your energy.

This book will help you understand many of the things you will be learning. At first, it will all be new to you. New people, strange language, unusual customs, and plenty of new movements to practice. Doesn't this sound like what you would expect if you traveled to an unknown land as an explorer? If we imagine ourselves on a mission to learn and investigate, then we won't worry if we don't understand everything at first or if we don't always know what to do and how to do it. In the martial arts, that is what your teacher and friends are for—to help you on your way.

Together, in this book, we will learn the meaning behind the traditions of the martial arts. Let the adventure begin!

chapter one
Why We Practice the Martial Arts

The most important thing to know about the martial arts is that they are healthy and peaceful activities. As you learn about their history, you will see that true martial artists do not want to hurt anyone or have violence in their lives. They work to not have conflict in their lives. They practice hard so that they will not have to fight and instead can show the strength and beauty of their technique in an artistic way. This is why it is called martial ART, not fighting.

If you play around at punching and kicking, you are not doing martial art. It's only pretend. To be a real martial artist means that you must pay attention to certain ideas. Learning them depends on you. What goes on inside your head is more important than what you can do with your body. How you think and the honesty of the smile on your face are as important as how fast your muscles work and how big a breath you can take. Experienced martial artists know this.

What Is a Dojo?

Many of you are already practicing martial arts, some of you perhaps for a couple of years. Most people go to a martial arts school or take classes at a community center. Some people practice in the park, and quite a few train in their own backyard or living room. Wherever you are when you study a martial art can be made a special place. A *dojo* is a place where you decide to learn and practice rather than just play. In Japanese dojo means "a place to learn and do." Korean martial artists call this a *dojang,* and those who study the Chinese traditions train in a *kwon.* You might call it a recreation center or a gym, which is short for the Greek word *gymnasium.*

Some people like to practice their martial art outdoors.

gymnasium
In early Greece a gymnasium was a group of closed and open spaces for students to practice swimming, boxing, and wrestling. Students also practiced other athletics and studied math, poetry, history, and important ideas in these gymnasiums.

In the forest or at the seashore, in a grassy field or on a rocky ledge you can create a dojo. Places where there is clean air and enough quiet to feel comfortable are especially good for learning. You may climb to a third floor of a building or down to its basement. It can be very plain and simple, and sometimes you may even have to imagine its boundaries.

The most important attitude in a dojo is *respect.* It is this respect that makes any dojo a special place. You must have respect for the space itself by deciding to make it important to you. If your dojo is indoors, it is important to keep it clean and neat. If your dojo is outdoors, you will be careful to not damage it or leave anything behind to mark it. You should respect the other people with you in the dojo.

Remember that your teachers work hard to teach you what they know and to keep you safe. Respect them because they are looking out for you and wish you well. Have respect for what you are learning because many smart and talented people have learned from good teachers and then passed it around the circle to you. Say thanks to those who have gone down the path before you, those who travel with you, and, of course, the students who come after you.

Don't be confused if you meet other people who have different names for things, different customs, and different uniforms. It may be that their school has a slightly different history than yours. There is a lot of variety in the martial arts and that is part of what makes them so interesting. All martial arts have something to offer. Make sure that you are a good representative of your school or style so that others will respect you as you, in turn, respect what they are doing.

Why Do So Many People Study Martial Arts?

People train in martial arts for a lot of different reasons. Many do it for fitness and fun. Others say that learning to focus has made a huge difference in their lives.

Fitness for Everyone

Martial art is good exercise. It helps to make us healthy and fit. We feel better, happier, and don't get sick if we practice regularly. It is important to attend your classes every week at a regular time, even if sometimes it seems easier to play with friends or watch TV.

Everybody knows that martial artists are strong and fast. Some of them can jump and spin in the air, do splits with ease, and break boards and bricks with their bare hands. They have practiced hard to be able to demonstrate these skills in front of an audience or in the movies. Of course, this is not all that they learn to do, but it makes a great show for people. It is a quick and easy way to make people aware of how they have been able, through practice, to train their bodies to do amazing things.

Martial artists don't have magical powers. They have learned how to apply the laws of weight and motion and knowledge of how the body works and how it can be improved over time by training. Performing these skills is fun, and having an audience appreciate their hard work is exciting. Most people, when they see a martial artist give a demonstration, wish that they could do it too. You may have seen a demonstration yourself or perhaps a friend has told you about someone at their martial art school who was able to do some pretty fancy stuff.

Everyone who studies martial arts learns to do things

that they have not been able to do before. Even if your school doesn't do demonstrations of jumping kicks or board breaking, you will definitely become stronger and your body will become more flexible. In time you will feel more coordinated than you did when you began. You will also find that other sports and games become easier.

Focus on Excellence

If you have ever looked through a camera, telescope, or microscope that had an adjustable lens, then you probably already know what focus means. At first your vision is blurry, but when you turn a knob or ring the right way, at a certain point everything becomes clear, sharp—in focus. In the martial arts we focus our minds to do something well. If you practice a certain way, concentrate on what you are doing, and feel good about the moment you are in, then you can bring your mind and body together to take a focused picture. It doesn't matter if what you are practicing is simple or appears impossible at first. If you think about a task in the same way and are careful to focus all your energy on it, then some day—sooner or later—you will be able to do almost anything you want. By learning to do something that seemed tricky at first in the martial arts, you can apply the same method to learning other things.

Fun to Learn

The ability to do martial arts well doesn't come all at once, and you were probably not born with it. Some people take longer than others to learn, and everyone is different. For example, spelling words may be difficult for one person, while addition of numbers is harder for another. Some people can draw a tree on paper. Others can only dance like a tree waving in the wind. In martial arts it is the same. People learn at their own speed. There will be days when your practice seems easy, and days when you have to practice over and over before you can get it right. You will feel great when you are able to do a technique well, and if you learn to smile gently at yourself when it's not quite working out, then even that can be fun too.

It doesn't matter if it takes you a little longer than other students in the class. They will have different successes and challenges to work on. Martial artists try to concentrate on their own progress and improvement—without comparing themselves to how their friends are doing. Many things can affect how quickly or easily you will learn something new. For example, how often a student can come to class and participating in other sports and activities outside the martial arts, can affect what happens in the dojo. Don't worry, you will walk your own path in your own time.

In a good martial arts class others will help you on your way. Although everyone should be friendly and want to help, it is important to pay attention to what the most senior students and your teacher have to say.

What Is a Sensei?

The teacher in a martial arts school is often called *sensei*. This is a Japanese word that means "one who has gone before." A sensei is like the leader of an expedition through a jungle or up a mountain who says, "Follow me, walk here, I know the way." As a student, especially someone new to the martial arts, you have to trust this person and listen carefully to his or her directions. It can be easy to lose your way at the beginning if you don't pay attention. Much later in your training, when you can see the path clearly for yourself, you may turn around to help others find the way by becoming a teacher. Some people even go off on their own and make new paths. It is in this way that new styles and schools of martial art are born.

A sensei then is someone who has practiced for a long time, studied martial art seriously, and decided to carry on the tradition by teaching new students. In the Korean language sensei is called *sabonim*, and in Chinese, martial arts students may call their teacher *sifu*. Teachers have different names depending on their experience and the school that they teach in. We call them by these special titles to show respect for what they have learned and the hard work they do in teaching their martial art to others like yourself.

When you meet a sensei for the first time it is important to smile, look him or her in the eye, and bow or shake hands if a hand is extended to you. Be friendly and polite as you would when you meet any new person and you will usually find that they will welcome you and be friendly right back.

This is especially true when you enter a dojo for the first time. Let's see what else you will want to know.

chapter two
Inside the Dojo

Visiting a dojo is like visiting someone's home. If we think of it as the home of the sensei, a person we respect very much, then it helps to remind us how to behave. You may have found that when you visit friends, your parents' friends, or other members of your family you discover different customs and rules. No matter what we do in our own home, we try to follow the practices of those we visit and be as polite as possible.

What if we don't know what to do? First, don't assume that how you do things is the way that it is done everywhere. Second, try to watch and listen for clues as to what is customary or usual at the place you are visiting. Third, if you really need to know something, a politely worded question to your host or someone else who seems to know the way around will often help.

You may find martial arts schools in many different places. No matter what cultural tradition the school follows, the training place is always special. In the Japanese tradition of the dojo that special attention begins before you arrive at the front door. As you drive, bicycle, or walk to the dojo, you should be thinking ahead about your class and what kind of energy you wish to bring to that special time. No matter how excited you are about training, always try to open the door to the dojo as a serious student of martial art. Even if you are just visiting you should show that you know how special the place is.

Somewhere near the door there will be a place for you to leave your shoes in order to keep the dojo clean. There may be shelves, boxes, or rows of shoes in a line. In some cases there may be small platforms or mats for you to step on once you have taken off wet shoes or boots. Try to *observe* where it is wet and where it is dry, or where it is dirty and where it is clean and keep it that way. Visitors to a dojo should also remove their shoes out of respect.

Traditionally a *samurai* always removed his shoes or sandals when entering a building. He placed them neatly outside the door, side by side and facing the way of his leaving. The samurai was always prepared to move if he needed to. Although not all martial arts schools follow the way of the samurai, it is always a good idea to leave your shoes neatly with laces or straps ready to be done up to go. It is said that a good sensei can tell how his student is feeling by how the shoes are left.

observation

To watch and think about what you see. To notice details and remember them. To see more than what you are looking for.

We show our respect for the school and our fellow students by not leaving our shoes where someone may walk, or in a way that they may get another person's shoes wet or dirty. Don't leave your socks in your shoes; take them inside with you to the change room. That way your shoes have a better chance to dry out on the inside. It can become very busy and crowded around the door if many students are coming and going at the same time. Don't be in a hurry—be prepared to wait your turn. Let the senior students change their shoes first. Try to arrive a little early so that you will not feel rushed.

Why is all this so important? Because how you act and feel when you come in the door of the dojo will affect how you train that day and how your fellow students and your teacher will feel about you.

Of course we all know that there are some days when you just don't feel like doing everything the right way. You are tired, or late for class, or just don't feel very good. A martial artist will tell you that those are the times when it is most important to pay attention to the little traditions like leaving your shoes neatly at the door.

Try imagining that you are leaving your problems of the day outside with your shoes. Whatever bugged you, made you sad or uncomfortable, does not need to come into the dojo with you. Take a deep breath and step inside feeling like you are starting a new day, a new time for you. In the dojo what you practice will make you feel better about yourself and it is your chance to make your class a special time in a special place. Wiggle your toes and put a smile on your face.

Keep those good thoughts with you as you change your clothes, greet your friends, and make your way into the training area. Don't forget to tie your belt carefully and make sure your uniform is in order before you leave the changing area. Also, wash your hands!

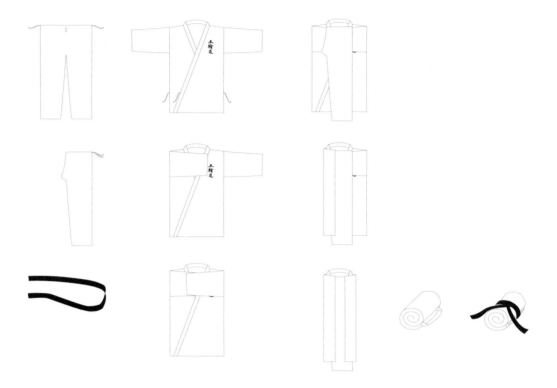

When you are ready and your teacher or a senior says that you may, enter the training area. As you pass through the door or just before (depending on the school) it is the time to bow. Usually you bow to the sensei or senior teacher if he is already in the room or you bow to the front of the dojo. In some schools a picture or painting or sign of some sort at the front of the dojo lets you know which way to face when you line up. If it is your first time, remember that you can ask someone.

Why Do We Bow?

First we bow to remind ourselves that we are entering a special place. A dojo, *dojang* or *kwon*, wherever it is, is a place to study martial arts, and if we want to be martial artists, we should think about it in a special way. The second reason we bow is to let everyone know (including ourselves) that we are ready to train. We have left our everyday thoughts at the door, we have prepared our minds when we dressed our bodies for practice, and we feel calm and happy. We are looking forward to what we will learn today. The third reason, which may be the most important one, is that the bow shows our respect to our teacher, our school and its history, and our fellow students. We are happy that they are there so that we can learn and practice martial arts. Never forget when you bow that you are a small part of a much bigger thing.

People have studied martial arts for many years throughout history and they bowed just like you. Different schools may have different ways of bowing. Their hands might be at their sides or joined in front. They may look to the floor or look directly at the person they are bowing to. These differences have to do with the history and the culture of the school, but their meaning is the same. One way to recognize a good martial artist is the quiet, careful way he does his bow. You can always feel that he means it even if it looks a little different from yours.

If you meet your sensei or senior student outside the training area you may want to bow to her if it is customary in your school. When you bow, whether it is to the dojo, your teacher, your friend, or someone that you are meeting for the first time, you will want to do it because you are telling them something, It expresses something you want to convey. Instead of saying it with words you are communicating with your actions. Although as a martial artist you will be expected to bow at appropriate times, it shouldn't be done just because you have to. Think about why you are bowing.

In the martial arts we are not trying to give a religious meaning to our bow. We are also not trying to say "I am your servant, master," which is a meaning that may have been true historically in some cultures. We want to show respect and understanding of our responsibilities, but we are not saying that someone is better than us; only that we are happy that they are there. Many animals bow to each other when they want to play.

When you bow to a sensei you bow to her experience with thanks that she is willing to teach us some of what she knows. Martial artists bow because they want to learn. They bow to those who have made it possible. Bowing is an international expression of greeting, beyond languages. A bow means that you will give of your best in return.

Lining Up

Most classes are taught with students in lines or circles. The shape they make is called a formation. Often they stand in lines with the most senior student at one end or at the front. The other students arrange themselves in order down the row to the newest student. If you are a new or visiting student, you always put yourself at the end of the line unless invited to stand somewhere else. It does not matter if you have trained before or wear more than a white beginners belt. It is important to recognize that you are new to this class.

Black belts often form a separate line to one side of a formation. They will ask to join the general group as newcomers if they are visiting a class or school that is not their own. The teacher will invite a guest to another place as a courtesy but will always make sure that he is in a position where he can observe how other students perform techniques or patterns that may be different to him.

Senior Students

We have described how a class will line up according to rank, from senior to junior student. Senior students have usually been there the longest. They may be a black belt or a colored belt that is more advanced than yours. They may be young or old, male or female. Usually those who have been practicing longer have learned more. Of course it's not the months or years you have been training that count but how much time you spend working hard in class. Some people are able to spend more time studying martial arts than others, so it is understandable when they move through the ranks at a different speed than those who do not study as often.

Senior students always deserve your attention and respect. They can be a big help to you in your training by answering questions and showing you the way. Sometimes they help the sensei by assisting her in teaching the class. These are the most senior students and are often called *sempai* to show that they work closely with the sensei to help improve the school. Occasionally a student with a lot of experience training and teaching will be named a sensei. In relation to the teacher who taught them they may still be considered a sempai. In some schools anyone wearing a black belt is automatically called sempai or sensei, but in others they have to be trained as teachers before they earn that title.

Always greet a senior, sempai, or sensei with a bow, and if they offer their hand to you, shake it with a firm grip and smile. No one likes to shake hands with someone whose

dojo formation

handshake feels like a limp dishrag, but also they don't like to be made uncomfortable by someone who squeezes too hard. Many people in the world say hello to each other with a handshake; others bow. Sometimes they bow and shake hands. You can observe or ask what others are doing to learn what is correct.

Every once and a while we do the wrong thing when trying to follow the customs or traditions of others. Usually though, if you have the right feeling or intention behind your smile, the other person will understand your true meaning and everything will be OK.

You can meet many new people when you study martial arts, which is one of the great things about it. You will make new friends along the way, both young and old. They will have different neighborhoods, schools, jobs, and interests than your own, and that makes it fun to share and learn with them.

The people that you train with in your own school will become very important to you. They are the ones who will be your practice partners and work alongside you when you are learning. You will practice your martial art techniques *with* them and sometimes even *on* them, so you must be careful to keep them safe and healthy. If someone is hurt or injured because you were not paying enough attention, then they might not want to train with you the next time.

Treat everyone in your dojo equally well. Even though there will be some people that you want to spend more time with as friends outside the dojo, you must have no favorites when you are training in martial arts. It does not matter where someone comes from, what clothes they wear, or what size house they live in. Inside the dojo what counts is what you learn and how well you try to learn it. Sometimes you will be surprised when you discover a person's true spirit. If you pay too much attention to how a person looks on the outside, you may miss who they really are and lose a friend you might have had.

When you know this, you'll work hard to make sure that the person you are in the dojo is the real you. Remember that a dojo is a place to improve or become better as a person in all ways, not just in the physical things you learn as a martial artist. How you think and feel about other people will be part of how you practice. Not everyone will be your best friend, but you can learn to treat all people with respect and courtesy and be smart about how we play and work together.

If you study and enjoy martial arts and try to be friendly and sincere with everyone, then things will usually work out. Try to practice with as many different partners as you can. You will learn more about martial arts and about other people. You will even learn more about yourself. If the custom in your class is to choose partners, then make sure you don't always choose the same partner. Don't let anyone be left out. Have the courage to train with everyone equally. If someone new joins the class, introduce yourself and make him feel welcome.

Bow to each new partner you work with. Show that you respect her and her willingness to train with you. Listen carefully to the teacher's instructions and make sure you are *always* in a safe position or at a safe distance when you practice with a partner. Never punch or kick so close to someone that you might hit him in the face or head. Don't even do it for fun because if you make a mistake someone could be hurt. It is always *your* responsibility to make sure that your partner is safe from harm and feels good about her time with you.

Remember that every moment you are in the dojo requires your full attention. Even if the class has not started or the teacher has to step outside for a few moments, you

sincere
To express honest, true, and positive thoughts and feelings.

discipline

The exercise of some control over your thoughts and actions, for health, safety, and enjoyment for yourself and others. To practice your mental ability to follow the customs of your dojo and to give quiet focused attention to your sensei.

should be on your best behavior. Anything less than that is unacceptable for a martial artist. Your teacher will let you know what you can practice outside the class time.

This time between classes is important to the martial artist. This is when he prepares for the intense learning ahead or relaxes after a good workout. This is not playtime, and although you may visit quietly with your fellow students, you should never do anything that may distract someone else from her personal time. If your teacher or senior has given you specific instructions, then follow them. Never practice your martial arts techniques unless you are properly supervised in the class. You may sit quietly until class begins or, with permission, do gentle warm-up exercises. By doing this you are exercising your discipline and avoiding accident and injury.

Hopefully all your partners will use the same care when they practice with you. Occasionally, someone may lose concentration or be feeling bad one day and you will have to be extra careful. If you think that his safety or yours will be affected, then it is important to speak up about it. Sometimes a person is honestly not aware that he is using too much strength, or going too fast or slow. Tell him right away if you feel uncomfortable. Let him know what is happening and ask him to change what he is doing. Usually that will be enough to make things better. If not, then you must

aware

To be awake, alive, and to feel with all the senses open. To be alert to all the possible consequences of movements you are making, and are about to make, in the dojo. To use care in observing the actions of your partners from moment to moment.

discuss the problem with your sensei and your partners. A solution will be worked out. Never try to use your own strength back at him. If you feel upset, try to understand what is really going on.

How Do I Behave in the Dojo?

We have talked about how special a dojo can be. We know that martial arts have a long history. They enjoy a tradition of respect that honors those who come to a dojo to train, including the youngest beginner. We act a certain way so that we can all stay healthy and safe and have a good time when we are there. We know that practicing martial arts is not the same as playing in a park, backyard, or parking lot. You may behave differently with your friends and school-mates than with your dojo partners.

Think about this: Instead of bringing your normal behavior from home or playground to the dojo, why not start treating your friends, family, and teachers on the outside with the same respect and courtesy you give to those inside the dojo?

Everything you say and do has an effect on how other people think of you. If you behave badly, people may think that you can't be a very good martial artist. They won't care how high you kick or how fast you can move. What they will notice is how you act outside the dojo, and that will matter more. Your teacher will expect that the attention you give in your training is honest and sincere and that you will practice that attention every day, all day, not just when you come to class. A sensei you may meet on the street or in another activity will usually be able to tell from your behavior whether you train well or not.

You may wish to bring a friend or members of your family to visit your school or dojo. They may come to watch a class or for a special event like a party, tournament, or grading. Make sure that they know before they come what to expect and what they should do. Remember the first time you opened the door? Let them know where to put their shoes, hang their coats, and where they should sit or stand. Let them know where the washrooms are. Always make sure that your teacher has given permission or invited them for their visit and introduce them when they actually arrive. Sometimes if many people are attending an event at the same time your sensei may not be able to meet everyone in your family, but you can have them meet the senior students and partners that you train with. If your guests have questions, they will feel more comfortable asking someone they have already met. Be a good leader for your guests and they will have fun. Remember that you are responsible for them and their correct behavior as well. Don't wait for someone else to give them instructions.

It may appear that there are a lot of rules about what you do in a dojo. Don't look at it that way. Think of all the fun and exciting things you are allowed to do because you have some guidelines to protect you. Having discipline and self-control in the dojo actually gives everyone more freedom to do martial arts.

chapter three
What Happens in a Martial Arts Class

Although you will find differences from class to class and teacher to teacher, most martial arts classes follow a basic pattern.

It is important to do a good warm-up before training with intensity. Some teachers say it is better to do a warm-up with no class than a class with no warm-up! Young people tend to be more active during the day than adults, but

intensity
To use your full energy to act with strength and focus.

their muscles and joints still need to be prepared with a warm-up. Martial arts techniques use parts of the body and muscles that are different from everyday playing and sports so you do special warm-up exercises to get ready. Professional and Olympic-class athletes and martial artists always take their warm-up seriously. They know that this helps prevent injuries and helps them get the most out of their bodies. The best performances follow the best warm-ups.

The teacher will then take the class through a review of the basics or *kihon*. He or she will help correct the way you stand, how you hold your body and arms, and the way you move from one step to another. Sometimes beginners have a hard time understanding why so much time has to be spent learning how to stand, when jumping and kicking is more fun. To explain this, let's take an example from building construction. At the construction site for a big building, the hole dug into the ground is huge and deep. So huge that many dump trucks and concrete trucks can drive around inside that hole. They are there to help build a strong foundation for the building. They use lots of concrete and steel, and sometimes they drill or blast through solid rock to put anchors in for the footings of the building. Now we may look at all this and think, "What a lot of trouble for something you don't even see!" But without that foundation, the building won't last long. Walls may crack, and floors become crooked. Bigger buildings have more serious challenges.

Your stance is the foundation of your martial arts technique. Your balance, strength, and the ability to move fast will all depend on good stances. How your feet are placed, your knees bent, and even whether or not your toes are curled will affect how you perform the simplest technique. You won't be able to do the fancy advanced moves at all unless your stances are near perfect. An opponent can knock you down easily if he sees your stance is not well balanced.

More seriously, you may get hurt practicing with an incorrect stance. Hips, knees, and ankles are meant to function well in certain directions. An injury can happen if the muscles and bones are pulled in the wrong way.

In the traditions of the martial arts, how you stand shows your character, dedication, and skill in your training. In old stories some of the bravest samurai warriors have backed away from fighting someone because of that person's superior stance—even before they drew their swords.

Your teacher works hard to teach you things in the right order even if it is not the way you prefer. Have patience. Many people before you have felt the same way. As they became more advanced, they were thankful that their teacher took the time to give them good "footings." Like a small child, every beginning martial artist, young or old, has to learn to stand and walk before he can run and jump. Your teacher will make your learning process fun and interesting, safe, and friendly.

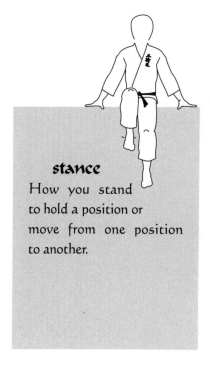

stance
How you stand to hold a position or move from one position to another.

When you are ready, and after learning some basic steps and positions, your teacher may start having you learn a *kata*. Not all styles of martial art have kata, but many do. The kata is an organized routine that students learn to practice combinations of techniques and to develop strength, speed, and flow in their movements. For some schools the kata becomes the highest form of training. It can be beautiful and energetic, and it is said that the true spirit of the martial artist is expressed in good kata. It is a chance to perform at your best, and it can be so exciting that it is possible to lose track of everyday feelings when you are caught up in doing kata well.

In some schools kata are done alone, and in others they are done with one or more other people as a team. They try to move together at the same time and with similar feeling about the movements. Like a dance, the participants are not competing with each other. Instead they are trying to join their energy together to create something large, beautiful, and breathtaking.

In fact when martial artists are synchronized with their mind, body, and spirit, they will find themselves breathing in and out at the same time! Good dancers and musicians find the same kind of union of energy when they practice and perform together. They sometimes call this quality "being in the same groove."

The grappling arts, like *judo, aikido,* and *jujutsu,* may not have patterns that look like the kata of *karate* and *taekwondo* because they do not do so much punching and kicking. However, these schools also have exercises with a partner that take a special rehearsed *form* (which is another word for kata). Each person knows exactly what she is expected to do and practice these forms over and over like kata.

Kata can also be practiced outside the regular class, although they usually require a big room. This is why many people practice their kata in parks. A common kata that is done outside is that of *tai chi*. Although it is generally much longer and slower than other kata we normally see in the martial arts, it is the same type of exercise. Many people practice the slow flowing movements to build strength and flexibility in their body and to improve their health. In China, where the practice of *tai chi* comes from, it is common in the morning to see hundreds of people practicing in parks or public squares. The movements are intelligent and beautiful, and if you speed them up a little, you can easily see that every move has a self-defense application.

Along with the warm-up, kihon, and kata, the martial arts teacher may introduce a new technique to be learned. That day's class may include some practice drills for the thousands of different combinations for the hands and feet that martial artists can perform. You can never run out of new things to do or new ways to learn something. With dif-

synchrony
To do something in the same time, with the same kind of feeling and energy. To move as one.

ferent teachers you will find even more variety in the way things are done in the martial arts. Learning may seem slow and simple at first, but if you practice your basics well and keep your eyes, ears, and mind open, you will be rewarded with years of fun and excitement in the martial arts. It's always hard work, but it's always worth it.

chapter four
The Tradition of the Belt System

Many schools of martial arts use a system of colored belts to organize what you are going to learn. Students look forward to changing their belts for a more advanced color. This is something like changing grades in school or levels in swimming. Other sports and activities have different classes like beginner, junior, intermediate, and senior, or basic and advanced. All these methods recognize that we can't learn everything at once. Martial artists discover that if they take things one step at a time they go slowly, but they go very far.

The color order isn't the same in all schools, but most begin with the white belt. A clean, new piece of paper is white and full of possibilities. You can draw, write, or paint anything on a blank page. The white belt is a very special time in the training of a martial artist because everything is new.

The colors usually progress to yellow, orange, green, blue (sometimes purple), brown (sometimes red) until eventually the student may be ready for the black belt. Sometimes stripes are taped or sewn on the belt to show stages in between colors. Some schools have meanings for their colors. Stories about the colors of the rainbow, seeds that grow into plants with the help of sunshine and water, and other images that help us think about the progress of our studies in the martial arts. It is said that the belt gets darker as the mind gets lighter!

Some schools that are more traditional use the white belt for a long time. When a student has practiced hard and is ready to accept more responsibility and demands in her training, she may be asked to wear the brown belt. This means that she is now ready to work at a high level where she must give a lot of time to learning, practicing, and helping to teach newer students. She must be a serious student because she is preparing to take her black belt exam.

What Does a Black Belt Mean?

If you take white light and shine it though a special glass called a prism, the light bends and separates into all the colors of the rainbow. In fact, that's what a rainbow is: white

You Can't Always Get What You Want

This can happen anytime: A hopeful student asks the teacher, "When can I get my black belt?"

The teacher looks the student straight in the eyes and says: "Five years."

"Oh, my goodness!" the surprised student answers. "That's a long time. But if I practice twice as hard, how long will it take me?"

"Ten years," is the quick response of the teacher.

"But you don't understand!" says the student. "I am going to try harder than anyone else and be better at everything. I'll do it quicker too, you'll see!"

The teacher, who has heard this before, slowly shakes his head and explains. "In that case twenty years, or maybe never." Seeing the disappointment on the student's face he adds: "Your head is too full of what you will be to the martial arts, not considering what the martial arts will be to you. Empty your mind and spirit to the flow of learning, and like a stream, let it take its course." The student has one more question. "How long can I study martial art?"

"Until you die," says the smiling teacher.

light shining through millions of water droplets that act like prisms hanging in the sky. White, which really isn't a color, contains all colors. Black is interesting because it, too, is really no color at all. Black means no light. Inside a box, a camera, a darkroom, or between the stars in outer space, it is dark and black.

How did white come to mean beginner and black mean advanced in the belt system? In the earlier days of the martial arts, students usually practiced with a teacher at their home, a farm, on the beach, or in a village square. The original *gi* or uniform that you wear today was just the clothes worn underneath a *kimono* or other outer wear. In China as well, plain loose-fitting shirts and pants were worn for practicing. These would be held together at the waist with a sash or belt. Buttons, zippers, elastics, and Velcro were not in use during these times.

The belt was a cloth folded over many times and stitched so that it would be strong and unstretchable. Sometimes students used the belts themselves to practice certain self-defense techniques. As a student practiced more and more the belt would change from white to brown, even after washing, and after a long time it would look almost black. If you were to see all the students of a sensei lined up in a courtyard, you could tell who were the more experienced or advanced ones by the color of their belts. This was the origin of the black belt—in truth, a dirty white belt!

Black Belts Today

Today's black belts are usually dyed cloth sewn over layers of white cloth. Now when black belt martial artists practice hard and long, their belt starts to fray around the edges and some of the white shows through. The more they practice the whiter their black belt becomes. Traditionally in the martial arts this is a good sign because it means that a person who has learned a lot is still ready and willing to learn more. In some schools they sew stripes on their black belts to show the levels of learning, or *dans,* that they are still passing through.

unique
Something special or one of a kind, unlike others. Stands alone as an individual.

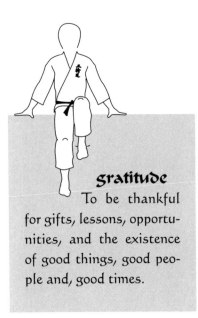

gratitude
To be thankful for gifts, lessons, opportunities, and the existence of good things, good people and, good times.

The black belt has come to represent an advanced level in martial arts training. It is not the end of the training, but another beginning, like graduating from high school and going on to university. Like college, there are degrees of black belt that continue on into the future as long as you wish to study. Some people devote their whole life to the martial arts, and if they become teachers or founders of their own school, they may reach 7, 8, or 9 levels or *dan* of black belt.

The martial arts systems haven't always been organized around the idea of changing belts. Some people think that today we have made the belt too important. It was never meant to be a prize. But because so much effort and learning goes into being ready to change belts, it seems like a reward when it finally happens.

You will find that many martial arts traditions involve circles. You don't learn in one direction or start at one point and move away from it. Although you may travel far, it is important to come home again to see where you started. When you begin again on the same path with more knowledge, you appreciate what you have learned and see things in new and special ways. You are also more able to help others find the path that you were on. Sometimes you will travel a different path, but you are well prepared to take on new challenges and adventures.

This is part of what makes your time in the martial arts unique and special to you. Even though millions may have traveled on the path, each journey is an individual one with its own experiences and efforts. What you learn becomes yours and is made for *you*. It doesn't mean that others can't own something similar. But what you let inside your mind and your spirit becomes part of you, in the same way that the changes your body goes through are yours alone.

We feel connected with other people who study martial art because we share the same excitement and interest in what we are learning. We help each other and show gratitude for the part we all play in the whole circle.

How Do We Learn?

You learn by doing. You learn by thinking. You learn by trying hard, by falling down a few times, and trying again. If you make a mistake, learn why it did not work well. The next time you try, it will be a little better. You can imagine what should happen and then compare the result with what does happen.

Mostly you have to remember not to worry if something doesn't work out the way you planned. Although some people may laugh at you, it is because they don't understand what you are doing. A martial artist will never laugh at or make bad comments to someone who is trying something new, even if it takes him many tries to achieve the good things that result when you practice.

The most experienced martial artist you know was not born being able to do everything he can do now. Even your teacher was once a white belt beginner and had to learn all the steps that you are learning today. If you are willing to work hard, you can go where your teacher has gone before.

Does the Sensei Know Everything?

Even though it might seem so, your teacher will be the first to tell you that she doesn't know all there is to know. What fun would it be if nothing were left to learn? Although it is good to be smart, it is not good to think there is nothing new for someone to teach you.

achieve
To arrive at a goal or a special accomplishment through work, study, practice or effort, and to enjoy the process of getting there.

challenge
A special difficulty to overcome or the setting of a goal that is not easy to rise to.

This can become a challenge for some people who become black belts, especially if they are teaching. It is not fair to expect a black belt to do everything perfectly. If your teacher makes a mistake, does that mean you shouldn't respect him? No, of course not! To learn to do something better, you have to allow yourself to make mistakes. A person wearing a black belt, no matter how good he is, is still a student too. He has lots to work on and to practice.

Sometimes teachers want to change how they do something to make their own students better martial artists. Just like you, senior students don't want to show off what they can already do well. They want to come to a dojo to practice and improve. We give them respect and space to do this. You also want this respect from them.

Belts and Titles

We cannot always tell how advanced a martial artist is by his belt or his title. Some schools have different requirements or standards than others. This means that a blue belt in one school may have studied different things for his belt, or in some cases the blue belt is a different step on the ladder. In Japanese we call the colored belt levels *kyu,* and they begin with the highest number, usually the ninth, and graduate to first kyu, the level before black belt. Sometimes a blue belt may be fourth kyu or sixth kyu in different systems.

This is one reason why you shouldn't worry too much about the color of the belt someone wears or compare yourself to others. Within your own school, it is easier to see how you are progressing because you know what you have to do for each level. If you are watching someone from another school and thinking you know more than her, be careful— you may be mistaken. Don't be quick to judge someone when you don't know the exact path she is following.

What happens if someone changes her belt before you do? This may happen because she has more time to train than you. She may also be physically or mentally more ready to practice the skills for the next level. If you think of your belt as a prize rather than something to hold up your pants or keep your *gi* top closed, then you may become confused. The colored belt should mean that you are ready to begin learning the skills for the next belt level, not that you have completely mastered the things that you have already learned. You will still have to practice and improve these older skills as well as learn new things.

Sometimes a teacher has to make the decision to keep a student at one belt level for a long time until he is ready for the next. He may be advanced in some things but need more work in others. Some of these areas may have to do with behavior or how well he understands his responsibilities as a martial artist. He may have high kicks or energetic kata, but he may not be paying attention in class or helping the younger students, for example. The teacher is probably not trying to punish anyone, but he can't, for the safety of the class and the progress of the student, allow this student to advance to the next level. Remember that your teacher is even happier than you when you are ready to change belts. It means that he has taught you well and now can teach you more!

Occasionally someone who started the same time as you will change her belt before you. Sometimes someone who started after you may also move ahead. Don't worry about it. Later you may change at a different time than her. Relax and concentrate on your own path. Also, if you change before someone else, don't start thinking that you are better. In the big picture, over time, it does not matter the color of your belt; what matters is how well you train. Stick with it and you will always improve. Remember that the black belt is a dirty white belt that has seen lots of practice and hard work. The colors are there to help you learn martial arts, not to hang on your wall.

Enjoy what you are learning today and do it the best that you can. You will find the same kinds of differences between black belts of different ranks. Second dan in one school may be like a fourth dan in another. The expectations and the work might be quite different. Many titles and names are given to people with high ranks. Someone who is sensei here is *renshi* there. Some teachers are called masters but not all of them truly are masters. We can learn more about someone when we see how many years he has studied and who his teachers were, rather than the rank he has earned.

This is why we should respect everyone equally for being martial artists and work hard to live up to the standards set by some very good teachers. How you behave toward others and how well you train in class will mean more to those masters who really know martial arts than the color of your belt.

chapter five

Demonstrations and Tournaments

How many sports can you name? How many of these sports have you played? Chances are your list may be fairly long if you have played sports in school or at camp, in the local community center or in the park with friends. In many sports people practice and play for recreation, not for competition. You can swim in a pool to cool off or you can have a race to see who can reach the end of the pool fastest.

You also can race for a school or a club. They may all be fun, but they have different meanings.

Martial arts serve the same recreation/competition purposes as sports. People have taken certain parts of martial arts training and made up rules so that students can come together and compete. Tournaments and demonstrations are a good way to make martial arts more popular by being open to spectators who watch and get interested in what they see. These events can raise money for school activities or community charities. The best competitions are well organized and have strict guidelines to ensure everyone's safety and enjoyment. Their whole purpose is to bring people together to share knowledge and celebrate the common activity in which they participate.

Are Martial Arts Sports?

Many schools in the martial arts do not participate in tournaments or competitions of any kind. Styles such as *tai chi chuan* and aikido hardly ever have these kinds of events, but in some schools of taekwondo, for example, they are popular. Taekwondo and judo are sports that you can participate in at the Olympic Games, a high level of competition. But it doesn't mean that everyone in taekwondo and judo competes. Some teachers and students in karate choose to make competition a part of their program, and some don't do it at all.

What Does Winning Mean?

Most sports and games are designed and organized so that there are winners. According to a special set of rules someone, or some team, scores more points, goes faster, or performs with more grace and *wins* the game. The other people (those who don't win) *lose* the game or event. Talented people who have practiced hard can win many times. Some win big competitions like the Superbowl, the Olympics, or World Championships and become famous.

Don't you find it interesting that very few people always win? Even the best have days when they are tired, ill, injured, or have equipment break. Even though they try their best, someone else has an exceptional day or gives a really good performance and wins. All champions have lost competitions and are still happy and proud to have lost because they had a personal best time or score or an experience that taught them a valuable lesson. Most just enjoy performing well, win or lose.

Everyone who participates in sports and competition learns that winning means that on that day, with that set of rules, and that field of competitors, someone got first place. Someone has to. That's the point of the game. On the next day it will probably be another who wins. Being a good sport means that you know the importance of playing well, following the rules, and having fun, no matter who wins. Everyone has heard, "It doesn't matter whether you win or lose, it's how you play the game." This idea is especially true in the martial arts.

What Is Good Sportsmanship?

If your school asks you to take part in a tournament, it is important to conduct yourself well and with good sportsmanship. As a martial artist you have a responsibility to show the highest level of respect for your fellow competitors, their teachers, and all the judges and officials. Respect for others is the basis of good sportsmanship. Remember that you are there to learn how to perform under pressure.

The trophies and medals don't always go to the person who has the best kata, fastest sparring skills, the highest kick, or the loudest *kiai*. The winner of a martial arts sporting event is usually the one who keeps his focus during the competition. It is easy to become nervous or distracted by all the people, the lights, and the noise. You need good physical skills to begin with, of course, but you will probably find that a tournament or demonstration in front of an audience is a great mental challenge as well.

Respect for Other Styles and Schools

If you attend a tournament, especially one of the larger ones, you will encounter martial artists from many different schools. At some open tournaments you may meet people who have traveled a great distance to participate. You will see different uniforms and different ways of bowing. We have talked about the many styles in the martial arts, like the variety of flowers in a garden or trees in a forest. No one variety is better than another.

In a performance of kata you may see both traditional forms that have been maintained for many years and new inventions set to music with costumes. Usually these kata are judged in different categories, but sometimes an overall champion is chosen among presentations that are quite different. This can be difficult for the judges, and audience reaction may influence them. Serious martial artists, especially those who have studied traditional styles, can appreciate the training and dedication that goes into learning and preparing a kata for a tournament. Others who are not as familiar may be more impressed by a performance that is not as difficult but has a flashier presentation.

In sparring competions and self-defense demonstrations, it is also difficult to decide on winners. The rules can vary from one tournament to the next, and judges may not always be fully aware of all the skills that they need to be looking for when they award points. Some schools require more contact than others, and many do not allow any contact at all, especially for young people. Make sure you, your parents, and your teacher are fully aware of all the rules so that you will know what to expect if you decide to participate.

Winning at a tournament should be less important than the inspiration and fun of coming together with other martial artists to share and enjoy different ways. Choosing winners often makes the other participants feel like losers, and this is not the point.

Not all schools have the same ideas about the meaning of competition. You will be guided by your coach or sensei when you attend a tournament. However, as always, your own behavior is your individual responsibility. Be a good sport and don't get caught in the trap of thinking: "My school is the best and anything outside it isn't worth paying attention to." This is the worst form of disrespect and is not how a real martial artist operates. Watch others to see what you may learn. Ask questions and explore new experiences.

Don't make the mistake of telling your teacher that you saw something done a better way. What you see is something different, and your own school and teacher have their own ways of doing things and usually good reasons for doing them. With respect in your mind for all martial artists, you will find the right balance between loyalty to your own school and interest in others.

Practicing Respect for Officials, Coaches, and Competitors

When you respect yourself and the traditions of the martial arts, you will have no difficulty knowing how to behave in a tournament. At the very least, you should act with the same careful, calm, polite manner that you maintain in your dojo.

With all the excitement and confusion at a tournament, it is even better if you are more formal than you are at your own school. It will help you to stay relaxed and focused. It will also remind you that, although you are in a contest, you are still a martial artist. It is not a baseball game that you have come to cheer at. Do not be influenced by the behavior of others if they are disrespectful or unruly.

Always bow before entering a competition area as you would at the door to your dojo. Bow even if no one else does. You are not doing it for them. You bow to remind yourself of what is important in your training and the respect you have for the traditions of the martial arts. Set an example and maybe others will follow. As a martial artist you should have the courage to stand on your own.

Always bow to the officials who lead your event. They may be called referees, judges, or sensei. It does not matter what title or rank they have or what uniform they wear. They are to be treated with the same respect as your teacher. Thank them for the time they are taking to help organize the tournament and to make sure that you are safe and have fun. Shake hands and look them in the eye with a friendly smile on your face. If you do not win your event and even if you disagree with the way you were judged by an official, still bow as you leave and act politely. It may take courage to hide your disappointment, but this is the type of bravery that you have been training for.

Remember that the person who is called your opponent in a competition should be your friend anywhere else. Do not forget that a tournament is a game, and although you should participate as a serious student, you must respect and be helpful to your fellow player.

Martial arts training teaches you that your attitude and your goals will influence what happens to you in any situation. You should talk with your parents and your teacher about how you feel about taking part in a competition. They will help you keep in mind what is really important: being healthy and having fun.

chapter six
The Responsibility of Being a Martial Artist

Responsibility

In the martial arts we believe that we can train to be a better person. As a young person you are still learning many new things. When you were a child, you had to learn how to speak, eat with other people, brush your teeth, and play games with your friends. You learned to share, say thank you, and be gentle with younger people and animal pets. These traits are all part of growing up with good character. Other people are then happy to be friends with you, invite you to their home, join you in activities, and teach you new things.

We have already talked about how important it is to behave correctly in the dojo. Let's look more closely at what personal skills, ideas, and attitudes we work on inside ourselves to be good martial artists. These are just as important as our stances, kata, and grappling and kicking techniques. Without them, our practice is empty and for show. It is not martial art. It is playing around.

character
What makes you special as a person, especially what you think, how you feel and act, and what you hold valuable.

You and Yourself

Martial arts help us learn more about who we are. When you were born, you were given a name to identify you. You have a birthday, a family, a school, and a community that you are part of. You may belong to a club or have a group of friends that you spend a lot of time with. All these things play a part in making you the person you are today. Hobbies, sports, and interests are also part of who you are.

How we think, what we think about, and the way we communicate with others creates the image of our *self*. If your name is Joe, who is Joe? Who is that person you see in the mirror? If you close your eyes and think "I am Ruth" (or whatever your own name is), you are thinking of yourself. If you say "I like ice cream," you are talking about yourself. If you are happy or tired or want to do something, this is part of how you feel about yourself.

You are a person. You have a right to be on this planet. Even though you are young, you still make choices and have your own ideas and opinions. As you grow, your ideas and

community
A group of people that works or plays together because they live in the same place, or they share interests, information, and resources that help the whole group.

society

A large group that may be made up of many communities. Though larger, the group still has things in common because of location, history, ideas, rules, values, etc. How a group works together to provide food, shelter, communication, art, commerce, and to protect the rights of individuals.

opinions will develop and change. Your family, friends, and teachers will help you find your way. They want you to be healthy and happy and able to be a part of society.

You and Others

Everyone is different. This is a good thing because if everyone were the same, life would be boring. People have different hair and skin colors, different kinds of bodies, speak different languages, and eat different foods. In the same way people have different thoughts. They may follow different religions or no religion at all. Many people live in cities and towns, but some live in the country or a jungle or a desert. Some people watch television all day, and others have no interest in it at all. They would rather read a book or go for a walk in the woods. Some people love and study martial art and some people have never heard of it.

People come together in groups to share good times and to work together. Despite our differences and disagreements, people need family and friends, enough food to eat, and shelter. We make rules or laws so that people can live together peacefully. We don't steal, lie, cheat, or harm other people because we want things to be fair and work well. We still have a lot of work to do before we can all live without fear, hunger, or disease.

Respect for Others

Practicing the martial arts is one way we can move in this positive direction, and it depends on each individual martial artist to help. If we each do what we can to improve our own lives and help others, those smaller parts can make up a great whole.

Respect others for who they are. Our teachers, parents, family, friends, fellow students, neighbors, and strangers all deserve our respect even when we don't agree with or understand their point of view. We want others to respect us, too, even if we have different opinions about things.

Respect your parents or guardians for what they have done for you. Remember that they want to protect you and are concerned for your future. If you make the decision to listen and learn what they are trying to teach, you will have more information and help when it comes time to make your own choices. Your family will respect you too when they see that you work hard at your training and that they can come to depend on you to make good decisions. Your friends are important people too. Give them respect and loyalty and be open to new people as well.

respect
    To see or think of someone or something in a positive way as special or individual. When you exercise respect, you will never have sore muscles from doing it too much!

Self-respect

What about respecting ourselves? Part of self-respect is knowing who we are and liking what we know. This doesn't mean liking ourselves so much that we think we are better than others. It doesn't mean that we think we should have everything that we want. There is a big difference between self-respect and being selfish. A selfish person only thinks about himself and asks the rest of the world, "What can you do for me?" A person with self-respect is comfortable with who she is, what she has, and what she can do. She can also say to the rest of the world, "What can I offer you, what am I able to do to help?"

A martial artist with self-respect stays healthy and avoids injuries. He knows that he can't eat candy and sugar all the time and still have enough strength and energy to train. He washes his hands so that he can avoid germs. He doesn't watch so much TV or play so many video games that his brain turns to mush.

With self-respect you learn to listen to your own voice and not listen to those who may want you to do something you know is wrong. You also won't listen to those who want you to be unhealthy or make you feel bad about yourself. You know that you are special but that you have lots to improve. You can laugh at your own mistakes and be proud of things you do well. Most important you don't have to make someone else feel bad so that you can feel good. You have learned that when you help someone else feel good about themselves, then you both feel better. You become a better person by being positive and looking for the good things in others.

Humility

Although it is great to feel good about what you learn and accomplish in the martial arts, it is also important not to become full of pride. It is natural to want to share your experiences with others, especially friends and family. But you don't want to make someone else feel less worthy because you need to boast about your achievement. Be happy but be humble. There is no need to boast. In return, enjoy the successes of your friends. Share equally.

A martial artist is humble because he keeps in mind how much more there is to learn. You will learn a lot, especially as a beginner, and continue to learn as you advance in your training. When you become a black belt, you will really know a lot. Even then, you should be the first to say, "I have so much more to learn." When you have learned this, you really do know a great deal.

This humility is part of the respect you show to your teacher and seniors. You congratulate them for the work they have done and the ability they have shown. You are grateful for their help to you.

We can never be perfect. After all, what would we do then, if we were? That would be boring! A martial artist does not practice to be perfect. He seeks to practice perfectly.

Integrity

Integrity is a traditional quality of the martial artist. It means to have a strong structure and foundation, to maintain what you think is right with strength and determination, to be yourself, to be whole.

Both the warrior samurai or *bushi* and the peaceful *Zen* monk represent these qualities. As martial artists you have difficult choices to make, but you train to have the courage to make the right decision even if it is not the easy one.

When you are young, your family and teachers shield you from some of these decisions. As a young martial artist you should be keen to see how things are done well. When faced with a choice, you should aim to be fair. When you can be more happy about being fair than whether you win or lose, you are exercising your integrity as a martial artist. This will affect how you think and feel. As we practice with our body, we practice with our mind and spirit as well.

Sometimes others will not agree with you. Occasionally almost everyone else will see things a different way than you. At these times you need to have the integrity to speak

integrity
To have the strength and wisdom to hold true to what you believe, not be blind to your mistakes or need to improve. To maintain your choices as an individual based on reason and belief, not because of the fashion of a group or others that may try to influence you.

Give a Little Bit

A student goes down the street to visit the tea master. This master welcomes students to learn the art of *chado*, the tea ceremony. This precise ritual is respected for its grace, order, and difficulty of execution. The traditional Zen tearoom is one of the only places the samurai warrior removes his sword.

Throughout the silent movements of the Zen master, the student asks many questions. He asks about the true meaning of life, how to become a master, why teachers answer questions with questions, why are there no windows in the teahouse, what is the sound of one hand clapping, why is the teahouse door so small, and is there any sugar for his tea?

Not noticing that the teacher has no time or room to respond, the student *does* notice that the tea master is pouring him his tea, and the tea is flowing over the top of the cup, over the table, and onto the *tatami* (straw floor mats). Shocked that such an experienced tea master has spilled the tea, he shouts, "Stop! What are you doing?"

The tea master answers, "Your mind is like this cup, too full and overflowing for any answers to pour in. Empty your cup and make a little room for emptiness. Be open so that what you learn can take the shape of your cup. Bow your head and make yourself small, like the door you have just entered, so that you can open your spirit to grow bigger."

The student drank his tea, turned the cup in a full circle, placed it quietly on the low table, and bowed.

your truth. You must keep your mind open, though, for you are not always right. A martial artist is not afraid to admit that he has made a mistake.

Honesty

Be honest with yourself so that you can be honest with others. Your feelings are often reactions to things that happen. They are not always how you *should* feel or how you *want* to feel. They may not even be how you *really* feel if you look closely. Being honest means looking deep within yourself, not believing every thought you hear. When you are honest with other people, it does not mean you blurt out loud every thought or feeling you have. When we speak, though, we should always take care to say what we mean.

We still have to be careful about the feelings of other people when we speak the truth. If you think someone is ugly, you certainly don't want to say that. But, you say, "I wouldn't be honest if I said she was beautiful!" We have to look closely at why we *think* she is ugly. Is it because she doesn't look like a model in a magazine? Could it be she doesn't look like you or your friends because she wears her hair a different way, or her body is different, or her clothes are different? She may see beauty differently than you do, and you may not have the experience or knowledge to understand that difference yet.

You as a martial artist must ask these kinds of questions of yourself first. That is being honest. The truth you speak after you look inside yourself will be stronger and more valuable. You will have many experiences in your life where you will have to think about what honesty really means.

Willingness to Learn

The best way for a martial artist to keep a good balance between pride and humility is to always be willing to learn more. When your teacher wants you to practice and work on something that you have done before, it is not because you were doing it wrong, but the time has come for you to do it better. Many advanced techniques are built on earlier simpler movements. Sometimes it is necessary to revisit these things that we have already learned to do and change them slightly so that they work better when combined in more complex ways.

For a time you may feel awkward or frustrated changing what has felt comfortable. This change can also affect how other techniques feel. This effect is natural and temporary. Once the work is done, it will feel much better and the results will be well worth your trouble. Being willing to learn during this period and not worry about how it looks to others will make it easier.

The ability to practice and improve is an important part of learning martial arts. It is also why you are reminded not to judge or compete with others. You may be watching them when they are working hard to correct something or include a new skill in their training. Think about how much more freedom you yourself will feel if you do not always have to protect your image or your pride. Be happy and open to learn and improve what you can do.

value
What is important and is worth something, although not necessarily measured in money. It can also mean what is right and good.

Dedication and Effort

In the martial arts, value is given to things that are not easily or quickly learned. We have talked about how some people progress more quickly than others. Everyone who studies martial arts will one day find a technique, idea, or method that at first they can't seem to get. For most martial artists this happens all the time, and then qualities like patience and paying attention get their own workout. This kind of problem won't be solved by punching harder or kicking higher. You must smile, take a deep breath, exhale, and dig in to your practice. Your teacher and seniors will help you, and as long as you do your part, they will be there for you as long as it takes. Some day it will be your turn to help them.

What is your part? "Just try your best" is something that you often hear parents and teachers say. They want you to know that whatever you do will be OK. But, you may ask, "What if my best is not good enough? I tried and I can't do it!" Sometimes you will feel like you don't want to try anymore. It is natural to feel this way, and you are not the first person to want to stop when things aren't working out. Most martial artists have felt this way more than once. By the time you are an advanced student, you will have had chances to see when you are having difficulty, you don't have to feel bad.

Mind Work

It all depends on how you think about it. This is a good example of why martial artists talk about training their mind as well as their body. It is easier for you to understand that you must hold your foot or your knee a certain way for a kick to work. When you are told that you must hold your mind a certain way, it's harder for you to know what to do.

If you decide to stop practicing something because you think you can't do it, then it becomes true that you can't do it. You stop there, not having done it, and if you don't try again later, well, it never gets done. Experienced martial artists will tell you stories of how they fell down nineteen times and then on the twentieth time it worked. They were suddenly able to do something that they couldn't do those nineteen times before. They kept trying, though, because they knew that eventually it would work. You will find out after this has happened to you a few times that you must believe in your ability to learn no matter how long it takes. When you decide that you *can* do it in your mind (even if you haven't done it yet) then you are many steps closer.

Positive Thoughts

A famous old master of martial arts told his student "There is no try, just do." What he meant was that you must dedicate your mind to positive thoughts. Even though his student meant well when he said he would *try* to do something, the teacher felt that that word allowed too much room for the idea of failure to enter his student's mind. Believing that you will *do*, even if it takes forever, is much better training for your mind. Sooner rather than later, your body will get the right idea.

Sometimes it doesn't seem easy. We want things to go fast and smooth and come out right. You need to remember that a lot of people will tell you that fast and cheap is good. Advertising, especially on television, wants you to believe in instant happiness. Advertisers want you to buy their product by convincing you that if you "just add water and stir" then you will have something better than something you made yourself. Does it really taste better? Fast food can be fun, but you don't want to eat it all the time.

Don't expect an easy ride from the martial arts. That would take away much that is special and valuable from what you can learn. Look carefully at what you have decided to do for yourself. Taste every bite and enjoy every step. No one else can have the same experience you will have.

Nowhere to Run

The sensei hung an inflated ball in the corner of the dojo so that the students could practice their reflexes with a moving target. One student danced round, dodging this way and that, usually missing the ball. He managed to hit the walls though, bouncing off and muttering, "This room is too small. We need a bigger place to train."

Hearing his complaint, the next day the sensei hung a heavy canvas bag stuffed with sand and cloth padding in another corner of the dojo, so that his students could practice hitting a target that didn't move. Another student ran and kicked, jumping in circles to make the heavy bag swing from its hook in the ceiling. "I need more room to give me momentum. It's hard to move this thing."

The next day the sensei hung yet another heavy bag in a third corner. "It's getting hot in here with all this running and bouncing. We're too close, we need more room," a student complained. After the weekend the students arrived to find a refrigerator filled with cold juice and spring water inside the dojo. Although they had to be careful opening the door of the fridge when someone ran by, most of the students reach for a cold drink. A new student complains, "My elbow gets knocked when I'm trying to drink. There's no room to sit!" For the next few days the dojo filled with chairs and more chairs, some that folded against the wall and some that had plush cushions. Now everyone sat and watched a few students who occasionally got up to hit the hanging ball. "I wish we had room to do kata," an older student said.

The next day (with general agreement that there was not enough room to practice), the sensei asked all the students to move the ball and the heavy bags and the fridge and the chairs out of the dojo and into the lobby. Suddenly the dojo seemed empty and full of possibilities. "There is so much more room here!" said the happy students. "I never noticed how much room sensei has provided us with to train. We should practice easily with all this room."

The sensei watched, sipping his water.

Dedication means deciding to practice well and sticking with it even when it isn't easy. Sometimes you have to make more effort than you have before. Think of what it's like to ride your bicycle up a hill. As you near the top, you have to breathe deeply and push and pull harder than at the bottom. Finally you make it over the rise. If you are lucky, the view from the top of the hill may be great. Perhaps that is why you decided it was worth the effort to climb.

Understanding Others

Martial arts training teaches you to be centered within your universe. This does not mean that you are the center of everyone else's universe. However, we do all share a universe together that we must respect and protect.

Understanding other people, other living things, and especially how the world is made up of infinite connections of molecules and forces of energy, will put you in perspective. You are a unique part of this universe. Remember as you encounter others in your life, that they have their own special part to play. It does not have to be the same as yours.

Martial artists traditionally have tried to learn about other people, to help them, and to work with them even if their views are different. To learn how a training partner or

perspective
The way you look at some thing, place, or person or how they appear from where you are looking. Sometimes what you expect to see, or want to see, can affect how your mind understands what you are seeing. Things can appear differently depending on size, distance, and what else may stand in between.

Inner Traditions • Bear & Company

P.O. Box 388

Rochester, VT 05767-0388

U.S.A.

INNER TRADITIONS

BEAR & CO.

HEALING · ARTS · PRESS

DESTINY BOOKS

Park Street Press

BINDU SKY BOOKS

BEAR CUB BOOKS

Please send us this card to receive our latest catalog.

☐ Check here if you would like to receive our catalog via e-mail.

E-mail address _____

Name _____ Company _____

Address _____

City _____ State _____ Zip _____ Phone _____

Order at 1-800-246-8648 • Fax (802) 767-3726

E-mail: orders@InnerTraditions.com • Web site: www.InnerTraditions.com

opponent will react, we must begin to understand the things he does. To practice with fellow students and teachers you try to respect their own goals and challenges as you work on yours. Listen to other people and their point of view. Change your view, if you like, to agree with new things you have learned. Explain to others how you feel in hopes that they, too, will listen and understand. You are responsible for what you choose to think and feel about others.

Pitching In and Helping Out

Alongside the responsibilities a martial artist has as an individual, you do things as part of a group. We have talked about self-respect and personal integrity as qualities that you can produce inside yourself. When you train in the martial arts, you are concerned with your own progress and not trying to compete with others. In most cases you do not train alone. You need your training partners to practice with, have fun with, and share your energy and enthusiasm.

Many people work so that you can enjoy learning about the martial arts. Your teachers work hard to offer a class schedule. There may be staff who keep your school or community center clean and safe for you to train in. Someone keeps track of paperwork—paying fees and insurance, maintaining memberships in associations, advertising in the yellow pages, newspapers, and flyers, and keeping information on the Internet and in brochures. You may think that these things have nothing to do with you directly, but all this work needs to be done for you to have a place to train and a teacher and class to practice with.

In most schools and clubs, students are asked to help with tasks. Usually senior students become involved with organizing events and activities. If you are asked to help out in some way you should be glad for the opportunity. Don't expect to be paid or rewarded. It is part of your training as a martial artist.

Traditionally students did all the work around a dojo; cooking, cleaning, sweeping, repairs, and so on. Even today in traditional schools there are *uchi deshi,* live-in students who share responsibilities in the dojo as a family does in a household. Even though there are not many people who are able to devote themselves so completely to their training, when we do go to the dojo we should feel the same.

There are many ways to help out, but we don't need to wait to be asked. When you see something that needs to be done, ask if you can do it, like keeping mats and equipment organized, dressing rooms neat, and garbage cans emptied. The less time your teacher or senior student has to spend on these jobs, the more time they will be able to spend teaching and helping students. Everyone benefits when everyone pitches in and helps out.

Helping Outside the Dojo

A martial artist will want to help others outside the dojo too. Martial arts clubs try to set an example in the community by participating in different activities. The club may organize a food drive or raise money for an important cause. As an individual you can help an organization, a friend, or someone in your neighborhood who could use a hand. Some people are able to pay for odd jobs, but there are many who cannot. A martial artist will not use money as his only motivation for lending a hand.

As you grow older you will be able to participate in more activities and contribute to your community and to society as a whole. This is a great responsibility as well as a great opportunity to make a difference in other people's lives. What you do will also make your own life richer and happier.

If you think for a bit you can probably come up with a good list of ways to help your family at home. It is important to do your share of the little jobs that always need to be done to keep your home clean and working well. If you help other people with their chores or errands then they might help you. You will have more time together to talk and enjoy each other's company. When the work is finished there is more time to play and do other activities.

Being Ready

In medieval times warriors sometimes had to help their community by fighting invaders or robbers who wanted to harm their people. Samurai warriors would travel great distances to fight in wars for other people that their master had promised to help. Even today we have military people who try to bring peace and end warfare in many regions of the world.

errands
Small jobs that are done on a regular basis to help maintain order, beauty, health, or a system of work. Often done in and around the home or neighborhood, or related to shopping.

The warriors of today also help to defend the health and safety of people who cannot help themselves. When a natural disaster like a tornado or earthquake strikes, military and volunteer personnel organize to provide assistance to thousands of people. Because they are trained and ready, they can be among the first to arrive on the scene with food, shelter, and fresh water. Emergency medical professionals are like warriors too because of their hard work, training, and the risks that they take to help others.

Being ready, like a warrior preparing for a battle, is different for a martial artist. It does not mean having a gun or looking forward to going out and fighting. It means being healthy and strong and organized. It means being willing to give your time and to suffer some discomfort to make life better for someone else. It means being alert and awake and looking around you to see what can be done. A martial artist is always ready to jump up with positive energy and good attitude. Taking care of your health so that you can do the best that you are capable of is a valuable warrior tradition that has been passed down to martial artists.

Thinking ahead is part of being prepared and ready for anything. Your training teaches you to know in advance what you are going to do and to focus your energy in that direction. Lifeguards, airline pilots, boat captains, and organizers of large events all have to plan ahead and think about what might happen. Sometimes accidents do happen and good preparation can make sure that help is nearby and ready to make things better.

Obedience and Personal Freedom

You may by now feel that a martial artist is always making decisions and choices. You may also think that there are a lot of rules. They may be about how to behave, how to think, feel, and act. As a young person, you may not feel that you have a lot of choices. Parents, teachers, and rules control most of your life, and things are not always how you want them to be. You are often told that you must be older or bigger or learn more before you are allowed or able to do something. Adults feel the same way too sometimes. Old people sometimes think that they are *too* old to do something and wish they were young like you again.

We have talked about how parents, guardians, and teachers want to help and protect you as you grow up. Other people such as doctors, nurses, lifeguards, police, and firefighters are also watching out for us. Our society has many rules to protect property, possessions, and people from harm. We also have to have laws to protect our natural environment from pollution, misuse, or disasters that happen by accident or mistreatment.

All these rules we choose to obey or follow, not just because there are punishments or consequences if we don't, but because there is good reason to do so. By accepting the limits placed on us by good rules we do not lose personal freedom, we gain it. Our world will be a better place if we can watch out for each other and nature and be more tolerant of differences. A martial artist is always trying to make a balance between what is good for the individual and what benefits the group.

Generally, you can begin to make more choices about your own path as you learn more and show that you are responsible. When you are learning in school and in the martial arts, set programs help you develop your skill. There are standards and levels or grades that you must finish before going on to the next. Sometimes you may want to go another way, but you won't be allowed until you can show that you are able to follow the marked path first. After that if you go out on your own, you are better prepared and more likely to be successful doing your own thing.

When to Ask Questions

Traditions and laws are guides to behavior that develop over time in society. Although these guides are necessary, there are times when changes should be made. When you are young, you have many questions about why and how things happen. You should try to find answers. A martial artist will be respectful when asking questions and listen to the answers carefully before asking more questions or forming opinions.

At times your questions will lead you to the belief that something is not right. When you speak out, be prepared to defend yourself with facts and good thinking. Knowledge and awareness do change over time, and sometimes we need people to help us open our eyes. Remember that at one time slavery was legal, but that did not make it right. People had to fight to change that law, and it was a difficult time for everyone. Recently we used many chemicals that we thought improved our lives but we did not know that they damaged our health and environment. Changes are being made because people studied the problem, spoke out and taught us new ways of seeing, working and living.

In the martial arts students learn that they have a place in society and that they must take responsibility for their actions. They learn to think and learn and practice many things and many ways. They learn to be more open to others around them and take joy in differences between people. We learn that under the surface we have much in common.

As a young martial artist you will do what you can do in your own world. Don't expect to be able to do everything, but if you can help out and do your part, you will be living up to your responsibilities. When many people do this all together, great things can be done. The world can change when people unite. We should be just as ready to do battle for good, right, and beautiful things as we are to work against forces that take away energy. Martial artists practice to make themselves better and the world turn in a positive direction.

chapter seven
What Is
Self-defense?

By now you know that martial arts are more than punching and kicking. It is easy to imitate a martial artist by stirring up the dust with some fancy footwork and letting out a few screams. This is often done in fun. However, if you have been reading this book up to now, or you have trained in the arts for a time, you know that this is not what real martial arts are. The next time someone asks you to

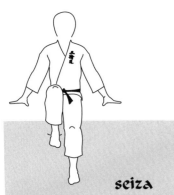

seiza

Most martial arts have exercises for the student to calm his or her mind and prepare for training. A typical class will usually include a short period of sitting quietly at the beginning and again at the end of the session. Those who train in Zen meditation use this exercise as their main activity. A student in a Zendo may sit in seiza for hours. Seiza means to sit in correct form, spine straight, head erect, hands and shoulders relaxed. The student begins the exercise by focusing on breathing, particularly the long, slow exhalation of air.

show him some martial arts you might just as easily sit in *seiza* with your eyes closed or take off your shoes and bow. This is more truthful but not as showy for your audience. A real martial arts expert watching your demonstration would know and be impressed with what you have learned.

It is true, however, that when you are practicing martial arts, there is a fair amount of punching and kicking, or in some styles, grappling and throwing. When you are more advanced, these techniques are performed with a partner. Are you fighting when you do this? Certainly not. Most martial artists will not use the word *fighting* to mean anything that they do in the dojo or even a tournament. A match or a sparring session better describes those training exercises. From a distance these may look like a fight but differ greatly from it in reality.

Fights

A fight happens when two or more people have entered a situation that is out of control. Emotions of anger, fear, and frustration are present and usually at least one of the persons wants to hurt the other. Fights can occur for many different reasons, but most of the time a fight can be avoided.

Sometimes fights happen because two or more sides can't resolve their conflict. They are so far apart and see things so differently that they can find no common ground. Usually both sides feel that they have been terribly wronged or something unfair or insulting has happened and that the other side is at fault. Many times, unfortunately, people will fight for no reason. They just get caught up in their pride, fear, or anger. Some people have learned this behavior from others and think it's OK. Others are just so unhappy or unwell that they can't help hitting other people.

There are one-sided fights too. Occasionally a person

will attack someone he doesn't know because that person happened to be there when he lost control of himself. Someone might attack another person to rob her or force her to do something. Fortunately this doesn't happen very often in most of our communities, and it probably won't happen to you. It is even less likely that you will become a person who would hurt someone else. For most of us, these things happen only in stories.

Battles and wars between communities or countries happen in the same way. Conflicting needs or ideas cause feelings of fear and anger to get out of control and fighting breaks out. Once the two sides have started hurting each other, it just gets worse and worse. The best way to end a fight is to stop it from beginning.

When two people are fighting, it takes an outside force to go in and break up the fight. Holding the two opponents far enough apart cools them down. When two dogs or cats fight, a cold shower with a hose can be enough to end the fighting. When large groups of people are at war, it is much more difficult to come between them, but it does happen. Peacekeeping forces and negotiators can help warring countries to stop long enough to search for ways to change the path they are on. Sometimes, like people, they need to want to stop hurting each other and being hurt. Eventually they become more willing to understand the other side. History shows us that it is better to try everything we can to avoid a fight. Once it begins, it is difficult to end it.

Give Peace a Chance

Usually both sides have to give something up to start making peace happen. Unfortunately in the world there are still places where so much fighting and suffering has occurred, and so much injustice still exists, that peace is very difficult to achieve. Nevertheless, many brave and determined people continue to work and believe peace will happen.

Many martial arts techniques originally developed during times of war. We will learn more about the history of the martial arts in chapter 9. This type of fighting was used only in self-defense when an individual or a community had no choice but to fight for their survival or the protection of their family and homes. Some of the traditions of the martial arts, such as loyalty, bravery, and tolerating pain and hardship have come from wartime. Most of the training and traditional ways of the martial arts have come about when these old societies turned to a way of peace. They organized themselves and developed codes of behavior that helped them control fighting and bring peace to the daily lives of their people.

Today we are fortunate that most of us live in peace most of the time. People who study martial art should be aware that this is not how it is everywhere in the world. Even in our peaceful society there are times when crimes are committed and people are hurt. In your schoolyard or in your family you may have observed or experienced some fighting.

People who train in martial arts are not fighting when they practice. No hate, anger, fear, or frustration is behind the moves they make. In fact most martial artists are good friends with the people who help them train. They have fun in the dojo and enjoy learning everything about the martial arts.

injustice
A situation that is wrong or unfair, where someone is not treated equally or in agreement with rules or laws.

Self-defense

In most schools students learn that some of their techniques may be used in self-defense if someone does try to hurt them. If a stranger made you go somewhere you did not want to go, or someone on the street or schoolyard decided to hit you, you would use a self-defense technique to stop them. Practicing self-defense means to avoid, redirect, block, or control someone's attack to prevent them from hurting you. It does not mean to win a fight, to get back at someone, or to hurt them more than they have hurt you.

It is possible that you will sometimes have violent feelings. As a martial artist you must control them. As you train, you learn ways to stop these feelings and even avoid having them in the first place. The strongest and most expert martial artist does not want to fight and uses a self-defense technique only if a fight cannot be avoided. He knows that this kind of situation will bring him closer to feelings that make him feel bad.

If you feel angry or upset a lot of the time, or find you can't control your feelings no matter how hard you try, talk with a teacher or a parent. These feelings do not mean that you are a bad person or that you can't become a martial artist. It just means that you will need more help learning to work with your feelings. In the same way that you may need extra help with your math, your reading, or your basketball shot, some coaches can help you with your emotions.

The rules and traditions of the martial arts help martial artists keep their minds and emotions in the right place. They remember the enjoyment they have working together *with* people, not *against* people. For example, when you are practicing with a partner, a focus glove, or a heavy bag, you never imagine yourself hitting someone you dislike. Even if you are just pretending, you allow thoughts and feelings to enter your mind and spirit that should never be there. You may be practicing or playing with your body, but you are not training your mind or feeling your true spirit. You are not doing martial art.

It is not always easy to be the perfect martial artist.

In fact it is probably impossible. A martial artist knows, though, that her training will help her and give her tools to build her character and her integrity as an individual. By practicing the traditions and teachings of martial artists who have studied for a long time, she can become a better, healthier person.

For a young person it may be difficult to understand why people fight or how to avoid it or stop it. Sometimes you can do nothing about it and it is not your fault. As a young person you may feel weak and helpless because you lack the physical strength and power of an adult. When you find yourself in a bad situation, it is important to protect yourself both mentally and physically. Do not feel responsible for preventing or stopping the fighting or aggression of others, especially if they are adults. They are responsible for that, not you.

As a martial artist you will never use what you learn to overpower someone, make him feel bad, or hurt him. You will be responsible for yourself and your own behavior. In rare circumstances you can use what you have practiced to escape or prevent an attack on you. Discuss with your family and your teacher when this might happen to you and what you can do. Thinking about it ahead of time will help you be prepared in case something does happen, but more important, it will help you avoid it.

If someone hurts you or makes you feel bad or unhappy in some way, it is important to tell someone else. An older friend, parent, relative, teacher, or police officer will be able to help you. Even if the person who hurts you tells you to keep it secret or threatens to hurt you more, it is important to tell someone else. You cannot fight this battle alone even if you are a brave young martial artist. The more afraid you are, the more important it is to get help.

Real and Fantasy Violence

We see many acts of violence daily on television and in computer games, comic books, and newspapers. Some of these things are really happening, and some are made up. Young people and even adults sometimes find it difficult to know or remember the difference. In a television show you may see someone stabbed or murdered. It has all been done with fake blood and other tricks used to make you believe that the story is real. When you see someone bleeding in a news story, you realize that this scene *is* reality and the person on the screen is living a real life like yours.

When you are playing, you may point an imaginary or plastic gun at a friend and say "zap, you're dead." Your friend doesn't die, of course, and you don't want him to. If you kill off all the monsters in a computer game and punch, kick, and somersault your way through the dungeon or jungle to freedom, it does not mean that you are violent or full of hatred. It also doesn't mean that you are a hero or a martial artist.

The martial artists in many fantasy stories, movies, and games spend a lot of time fighting and little time training or leading normal lives. Sometimes when we see real martial artists, we forget that they are different from the fantasy martial artists. Even if they are greatly skilled, we may be disappointed because they don't have magic abilities.

What Is Real about Martial Art Movies?

Despite the fake blood and the special effects, some martial art movies have interesting stories: learning courage, good battling evil, and recognizing truth in yourself. There is a tradition in the martial arts of telling stories to show students how to behave, how to practice, and how to make good choices. We have included some of the most popular stories in various chapters of this book.

Martial arts movies have their own traditions too. Many films are made in Asia, where they are popular and include historical stories and figures from myths and legends. They have a recognizable style and sound and often include gymnasts using hidden trampolines to fly through the air. Some of the Asian stars, directors, and producers are also making movies in the United States and greatly influence what we expect from our martial arts movie heroes.

Even though by careful editing and special effects, the heroes are capable of superhuman feats of strength and agility, the actors who play these parts are often skilled martial artists. Some of the best are able to perform all their techniques in real time without much editing. Of course, they continue their serious training outside the world of cameras.

It is natural for a young martial artist to imitate these figures when at play. Be careful, though, not to confuse fantasy with reality when applying yourself to your own training. You may find that people who are not involved in the martial arts may have little understanding of what you do when you practice. Their only experience with the martial arts may be what they have seen on film. You will help friends and family learn more about the training by the example you set. A teacher watching you pretend to kick a fellow schoolmate may misunderstand your intentions or be concerned that you may hurt him by accident. When you are practicing in the dojo, you exercise in a controlled way and pay close attention to what you do. Outside on the playground, there are distractions and in the fun of the moment someone, including you, could get hurt. It is best to save your martial arts techniques for the dojo.

If you are asked for a demonstration or you wish to share your enjoyment of the martial arts with others, you may choose to perform a kata. You should ask your martial arts teacher about these requests and see what his suggestions or concerns are.

Cool Ways to Defend Yourself

We hope you will never have to defend yourself from villains and thieves in your real life. As a martial artist you work to avoid these types of situations. Many ways remain for you to use your martial arts training to protect yourself

Smoke on the Water

The student asked the teacher. "How should my mind be when I practice a martial art?"

The teacher answered, "Your mind should be like the reflection of the moon in the water. It is not the moon, which in itself is far away. It is the light of the sun reflecting off the moon and shining on the water. It is not the water, yet when the wind blows its image moves upon the water and then is still."

The student asked again, "In the day, when the sun and the clouds reflect on the water, you can dive into the sun. What other sun can we dive into?"

"Yourself," was the answer.

from harm. Remember that the main reason for all the punching, kicking, and grappling is to learn how to use your body and mind together. The exercises help you to become strong and flexible. As your fitness improves, you become healthier and able to defend yourself from germs and sickness. As your reflexes become faster, you are able to avoid injuries when you are playing sports or crossing the street. As you learn to relax and focus your mind, you handle your feelings better and feel good about yourself and the people around you. These self-defense techniques are very valuable in your everyday life.

Most martial artists learn along the way that it doesn't take much for them to be happy. People everywhere around the world want enough food to eat, shelter, healthy bodies, and friends and family. We learn to appreciate the natural beauty of our environment and become interested in arts and music. We look forward to learning new things about ourselves, other people, and the world around us. These are the things that we want to protect in our world, not possessions.

Although it is fun to imagine having fancy cars, clothes, and lots of money, these possessions will not make you happy or particularly special or original. Commercials on television tell you that you've got to have something or you're just not cool. Remember that they just want to sell you something. Tomorrow it is something else that you just can't live without.

Remembering what is important helps you keep your guard up and focused on your goals. Times in your life will come when you will have to fight to protect yourself or something you believe in. This fight will not be with your fists and feet but with your mind and spirit. A healthy body gives you the energy to carry on, but you may have to defend yourself in emotional and spritual ways. By standing up and speaking out when others disagree, by speaking the truth even if others want you to lie, by helping others to learn, and by being centered and honest with yourself, you can defeat enemies bigger than you. This is real self-defense.

chapter eight

How to Apply What You Learn

One of the most important lessons that the martial arts teaches you is to take one small step at a time. You know you can't eat an apple by putting the whole fruit in your mouth. You must eat it one small bite at a time.

The martial arts also teach you to keep focused and stay calm. They teach you not to waste time. You learn that if you apply your energy in one direction you can do something well and efficiently and then have more time to do other things.

You can apply what you learn in the martial arts to many parts of your life. The martial arts can help you learn anything you set your mind to. You can use these skills to improve your school work and your performance in sports. These techniques can help you in your everyday life. They can help you calm down when you are angry or unhappy, help you concentrate on a problem—even help you lift a heavy object!

Calm, Cool, and Collected

There are several techniques used by martial artists to help them stay calm and concentrate. These techniques use the breath and sound to focus the mind.

Meditating

Modern martial artists practice meditation to stay calm. They sit quietly before and after a practice session or class to calm their mind and separate the time for training from the rest of their day. They close their eyes and breathe slowly. They think about their breathing and sitting, with their backs straight and their shoulders relaxed.

There are different ways to meditate. Some people hum a musical note or say something over and over until their mind becomes still. Some people imagine places where they feel good or calm or special or strong.

Martial artists do this, too, but usually when they meditate, they are trying to empty their minds to feel clear and relaxed. When you try this, you may at first find that many thoughts about your day, or yesterday, or tomorrow pop

Breathing

Martial artists learn that breathing well is the most important technique that they can learn. The body absorbs oxygen from the air and uses it to feed the internal energy. This process of respiration gives back carbon dioxide to the atmosphere when we exhale. In order to make the best use of this reaction we have to fill our lungs. When done correctly the abdomen will expand slightly rather than the chest. We sometimes call this breathing from the abdomen or from the diaphragm (a muscle that separates the internal organs of the chest from the abdomen). This type of breathing is what singers, wind instrument players, and swimmers also do.

into your mind. It's like the random bits of talk and music you hear as you search for someting good on the radio. This is normal and should slow down as you remain quiet and listen to yourself breathing.

This is an important martial arts technique that you can use to calm down when you feel excited or nervous or unhappy. It can take time to learn, but you always feel better even if you only try it for a few breaths. If you find yourself feeling angry or upset about something, you can take a deep breath, let it out slowly, and then do it again before you speak or act in an unpleasant way. It is satisfying to practice your martial arts this way and know that you are learning something valuable to you. You will realize that you can use this everywhere in your life.

Concentrating

Martial artists use a similar technique to learn how to concentrate. You start by paying close attention to how you breathe out. By exhaling slowly and smoothly each time, you begin to control how your body responds to activity in the mind. You will begin to see the effects on the work you ask your body to do. You practice this technique sitting first, then standing and walking. After a while, you'll notice how you are breathing all the time. By letting your air out at the same moment that you do a move, like a block, kick, or throw, you will be concentrating your energy into that move. You can jump, roll, lift, or push the same way.

You are stronger when you exhale than when you inhale. If in your mind you can imagine that breathing out is like water flowing through a pipe or electricity through a wire, you can feel even stronger.

You can use the same technique to concentrate outside the dojo. You may be trying to draw a straight line or push thread through the eye of a needle. You may be trying to keep your mind on a math problem or trying to remember the name on a map. If you let yourself relax and focus on your breathing, your senses become clearer and answers come more easily. When you need more energy or feel tired or sleepy, you can also use your breathing technique.

Kiai

If you exhale your air quickly and completely with a sound, you are making a *kiai*. This shout helps you concentrate your energy in a short time. It is useful if you need to lift something heavy, or open something that is stuck, or break a stick for campfire wood. When you are running somewhere and feel out of breath, a good kiai can help your breathing and make your spirit stronger and lighter. Smile,

kiai

Kiai is a Japanese word made up of two smaller words *Ki* and *Ai*. *Ki* means energy and *Ai.* means union or harmony. When martial artists use Kiai they are uniting their own energy with the action they want to take. The shout that may accompany the action is an expression of Kiai that we can hear.

sing, or whistle when you are doing something difficult and this will help too.

Martial artists use the same practice to deal with feelings of anger or fear or worry. Sometimes you cannot change what makes you feel upset, but with a little effort you can change how you feel about what is happening. You know the way you can change the station on the television or radio if you don't like what is on? Martial artists try to change their attitude to feel better. It is part of self-defense technique, and it takes practice like all the other techniques that you learn.

attitude

The position of an object in space in relation to something fixed, like the wings of a plane flying in the air and their position to the horizon or the ground. We more often use the word to describe how we hold our mind and feelings in relation to a subject or a person. When we change our attitude, we move in the same direction but in a different way or position.

School, Sports, and the Arts

The techniques you learn in martial arts to concentrate and stay focused can help you learn new things in other areas of your life. You can use them in your schoolwork—either learning a new subject or improving a subject you are weak in. You can use them in sports and in the arts.

School

Your regular school may seem quite different than your martial arts school. They are both places to learn, but they differ in size and traditions. Your experience in martial arts teaches you to respect all your teachers for the work that they do to expand your mind and guide you on your path. If you pay attention, study hard, and apply your energy, you will do well in subjects that may have given you difficulty before. Remember when you began your training, things that seemed almost impossible you can now do quite easily. The same is true of other things in your life.

Sometimes you need to look at your problem in a different way to begin to understand. Sometimes if you ask the right question or ask someone to help you, things suddenly make sense. Don't be afraid of trying new things or tackling challenges that may appear difficult. You don't always have to be naturally good at something if you are ready to apply yourself and practice hard.

Later in your life you use these same skills to train for jobs and careers. You may also use what you know about learning to teach others.

Sports

You will find ways that your practice of martial arts will improve your performance in sports. Many professional and Olympic-level athletes train in some form of martial arts. They know that it is excellent for balance and coordination, muscle strength, and flexibility in the joints. They also appreciate how it keeps them focused on their competition. They learn skills to concentrate and stay relaxed under pressure.

Walk Between the Raindrops

The teacher said, "Two people went for a walk. It was snowing. One person didn't get wet. How can this be?"

One student answered, "One person was wearing a waterproof coat."

Another student replied, "It was so cold that the snow stayed frozen on their clothes."

Another student suggested, "Perhaps one was walking in the open and another under the shelter of the trees."

The teacher shook his head and said, "You are all concentrating on the statement one person didn't get wet. So the truth is avoiding you. If I said one person didn't get wet, does it not mean the two of them both got wet?

"If we think too much about the words and not what the words are pointing to, we can be confused and not learn the truth. After all, snowflakes fall where they should."

Like martial artists they want to achieve excellence and create special moments.

You will learn to respect your fellow competitors and teammates for what you can learn from them and for the opportunity to participate in the same sport together. Many top competitors are good friends even though they play against each other. Your training helps you keep in mind that how you play is more important than what you play. Although winning is nice, it isn't necessary for having a good time. Depending on your attitude and your goals, it may not matter at all. Quality of play, good shots, good moves, great saves, and laughter and excitement are what we remember long after scores are forgotten.

Artistic Activities

When you train with good energy and a clear mind, you discover that you can be more creative. You have new ideas and see things in the world around you that you didn't notice before. Part of what you learn in the martial arts is to empty your mind of clutter, like cleaning out a closet. Instead of thinking only about yourself, you want to look outside to see what is happening. You learn new skills and use them to express your own ideas. You feel more comfortable with yourself and not afraid to let others know what you are thinking.

It is traditional for martial artists to take an interest in artistic elements of their culture. The samurai of early Japan appreciated painting, poetry, flower arranging, and brush writing. They often practiced these arts to calm their minds before a battle and to remind themselves of the beauty and freedom they would be fighting to protect. The arts that we enjoy today may look different and require different tools or instruments, but they create similar meanings. We want to communicate our thoughts, feelings, and ideas using pictures, words, and sounds. In martial arts we use our minds and bodies to move with strength and excellence. All artists search and work for a measure of quality in what they do. To do anything well is an art.

Like the martial arts, you need to practice basic skills in the arts. Even the most talented singers or dancers were not able to do much when they first started. Natural talent helps, but their work and dedication made it possible for them to do what they can do today. Choose the activity that

What Is Art?

We have talked about martial arts because of their strength and beauty and how you as a martial artist are a part of passing on the art to others. For centuries the idea of moving the body exactly and with clear energy has been practiced as an artistic activity. It is not as easy to point to, as a painting or a piece of music is, and say, "That is art." We still can understand it that way. Arts like dance and theater may happen for only an hour or so. You cannot hang it on a wall. You may take a picture of one moment and hang that photo on the wall. It can help others see something special in what the artist is doing, but it is not the art itself.

best suits your character and talent. It may not be what you first try but don't give up too quickly. Enjoy each step and the rewards will flow, including some that you have not yet imagined.

The Individual and Being Excellent

By helping you to learn, feel good inside your body, and put your energy toward things you want to do, martial arts improve your life. With good tools you can build almost anything. Whatever you are interested in will become better the more energy you give it. Martial arts help you direct your energy in the right places and have the strength to carry on even if you become tired or discouraged.

If you decide to be good at what you do no matter how much effort it takes, you probably will. You do not have to be the best at it to still be very good. If it makes you feel good and it has value of its own, it does not matter if other people choose to do something differently.

If you are working together with other people toward a goal that you all share, you'll need to adjust your ideas or methods so that the team can do something together. Usually team members agree on what they want to do. They have to work out with each other what each individual can give to the project. Being excellent then means being good as a group, not as an individual. A leader or a coach helps everyone keep on the right track. A martial artist learns that she can put her personal goals aside for a time to help others achieve their goals.

Darkness on the Edge of Town

A martial arts student traveled to a famous *Kyudo* (Zen archery) dojo in Hawaii. He asked the sensei if he would consider teaching him what he could about making the arrow hit the target. The sensei rose from where he had been kneeling, raised his bow high in front of him, and slowly lowered it to his expanded chest. He drew the string and let the arrow fly. A moment later, it quivered in the center of the target.

"Awesome!" said the student. "You must be the best archer on the island!"

"I don't think so," said the sensei. "My teacher is a fine martial artist and taught me all I know."

"Perhaps I should visit him!" announced the student.

He crossed to a nearby island seeking out this amazing Kyudo master. He was interested to find the sensei was an old woman who drew the bow with grace and strength and let the arrow zing to the center of its target.

The student, without thinking, applauded slowly and said, "That was great! What more can you teach me that your other student did not learn?" The sensei raised her bow again with a new arrow and led her mind to the place where the previous arrow was. The arrow flew and split the first arrow.

"Wow!" exclaimed the student. "I must learn from you! You are the best!"

"Unlikely," replied the sensei. "I suggest you see my teacher on the other side of this island, beyond the mountain."

The student hiked for days to find an old man living in a small cabin in the hills. He arrived at night to find the sensei tending a small fire outside, the only light for miles.

The student inquired about the secrets of this teacher's art. The sensei rose from the fire and let an arrow fly into the darkness. "A leaf falls in the night," was all he said. The student lit a lantern and walked through a field to find a maple tree at the edge of the woods with a leaf pinned to its trunk with the arrow.

The student was astounded. "How could you have shot this leaf in the dark? How could you see?" he demanded.

"I closed my eyes," said the sensei. He bowed and sat back down at his fire.

chapter nine
Where the Martial Arts Came From

Most of the modern martial arts have their roots in Asia. These arts are mental as well as physical. This means that we study what is going on in the mind as well as the body.

Tao: The Root of the Martial Arts

One of the great thinkers, or philosophers, of Chinese history was a man named Lao-tzu. He had many wise things to say about how people think, learn, and live together. Lao-tzu is thought to have included the philosophy of earlier thinkers, as well as his own, in his book the *Tao Te Ching.*

His ideas became so important that millons of people made them part of their way of life. Many books have been written about what he called the *Tao* (rhymes with how). Tao was not the only philosophy being talked about and taught in China. The sayings of Confucius were also important in history and in the laws and culture of this area of the world.

These ideas traveled with monks to nearby countries after the sixth century in which Lao-tzu lived and taught. Many ways of teaching changed to include his philosophy, which became known as Taoism. Martial arts are examples of this change—and many other arts such as painting and poetry. Even flower arranging and tea drinking became important because they followed the Tao.

Tao means the Way. Although the Tao or *Do* (in Japanese) is often described as a path, it is also recognized as a circular path. The flow of the world around us, the cycles of nature and the universe, turning like a wheel, are ideas of the Tao. In Japan they call the same idea Do (rhymes with go).

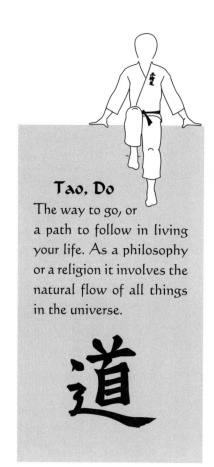

Tao, Do
The way to go, or a path to follow in living your life. As a philosophy or a religion it involves the natural flow of all things in the universe.

道

The Founding of the Martial Arts

Many people have shaped martial arts as we know them today. Some are well known and some not.

Bodhidharma and Chan

Written records tell the story of a man named Bodhidharma who traveled from India to China in 520. They say he was a Buddhist monk who wanted to teach people about the Buddha. The Buddha was a person who became loved and revered for his teachings and his life story. His story and philosophy became a religion for his followers to guide their lives by and make choices and rules.

Bodhidharma visited a Shaolin monastery in China around the sixth century. He taught the monks techniques that they could use to defend themselves without weapons. They developed an exercise system with these techniques to improve their health. They also studied meditation and the teachings of philosophy and religion. The temples were organized as schools, and the young monks were given difficult training and tests of their mental, spiritual, and physical abilities.

When the Shaolin monks learned about Buddhist teachings, they combined those ideas with their own Taoist beliefs. These combined ideas became known as *Chan*, a philosophy that is the basis for martial art traditions. Later, Chinese monks carried these ideas to Japan where the philosophy became known as Zen.

Modern Founders of Martial Arts Traditions

Even some of the more modern martial arts masters, sometimes called philosophers, lived more than four or five hundred years ago! Musashi and Sun Tzu are two names martial artists recognize as stars in the traditions of the martial arts. They are best known for teaching strategy or how to think your way through a game or a battle. They were warriors who were also concerned with peace.

Most of the well-known modern martial arts are around one hundred years old. The founders of these schools studied martial arts that were older. They made some changes so that more people could learn and improve their lives through martial arts. They still wanted to teach techniques and ideas that had ancient roots but in a way that would be organized, peaceful, and easy to learn.

Three of the most important masters of modern martial arts are Gichin Funakoshi 1868–1957 (*karate-do*), Jigoro Kano 1860–1938 (*judo*), and Morihei Ueshiba 1883–1969 (*aikido*).

Morihei Ueshiba became interested in philosophy and how important peace was to the person who practiced martial art. His philosophy was based on the ideas of religion and thinking that affected him. He gave it a great deal of thought and study. Later in his life he wrote and taught about his own school of martial art, which became known as *aikido*, or the "Art of Peace." He believed that the practice of martial art taught us about using energy in our bodies, our minds, and the world around us as positive force. It helps us understand others and turn negative directions away, or change them into good energy. This universal energy is known as *ki*. The Chinese language has the word *chi* for the same idea.

strategy
An idea or plan to make a number of things happen in the right time and the right order. A strategy is often used in a game or a battle or in organizing a business or a large event.

The Variety of Martial Arts

We have learned about the long history of martial arts. We know that there have been many teachers and even more students. They have passed their knowledge and experiences down through time, like a special present that is cared for and given again to another.

We can think of all the martial arts as part of a great tree that has many roots in the past and many leafy branches in the present and future. There are some big branches, just as there are major schools of martial art. Many small branches have interesting and unusual names that you may not have heard. If you haven't met a student of that school or read about them in a book, you may never have known that they existed.

Some of these styles are parts of bigger organizations and some are completely different and taught on their own. If you were able to watch a class they might appear to be doing the same exercises that you do. This is often true, but what makes them different might be in their mental training, the order in which they learn things, or whether or not they participate in competition. Sometimes they have learned from different teachers with special histories.

How Differences Develop

Schools can have differences within them too. Karate-do has its roots in a collection of islands close to Japan. The Ryu Kyu islands include one called Okinawa. On that small island there are many styles of karate with different names. How can that be? Some people trained with one teacher and they practiced on the beach in the deep sand. Others trained with another teacher who lived on the side of a mountain. Their karate stances and movements look different from

The Hwarang

The hwarang were the young warrior class of the ancient feudal Korean society. Little is known about when their organization began. Although the samurai receive more popular attention today in legend and published histories, the hwarang also have honored traditions and a love of the arts in the same way. They too were skilled horsemen and swordsmen and fought to defend their families and communities during difficult times.

each other because of their different environment. They had to change for the conditions of their dojo. Their style may have taken the name of their teacher, and it was passed down as a tradition within a family or *ryu* (school). Many of the people of Okinawa are fisherfolk or farmers, and for them it was important to practice using their tools. These became the *tonfa* and *nunchaku*, for example, that some schools practice kata with today. The oars from their boat became the *eku-bo*.

These kinds of differences exist in all martial arts both in the past and in the present.

Budo

There are many styles of martial arts whose names end with the Japanese word Do. Judo, aikido, taekwondo, and kendo are examples of this. Karate is a short form of karate-do. Do is half the word dojo. Since this word appears so often, it must be important to martial artists. An easy meaning to remember is how to go, or the Way. We can also think of it as the way to learn and live.

budo
The Japanese character describes an important idea for martial artists. It means the way or path to stopping conflict, war, or aggression.

Another word that you see in books about the martial arts is budo. It is made up of the two small words bu and Do. We have already learned that Do means "the way" in Japanese. Here is a picture word (or *kanji*) that describes Do. In these cultures the language is written with pictograms rather than the letters you are reading on this page. The brush strokes that make up this picture or pictogram have meanings and messages too. You can change the meaning of a kanji by adding or taking away strokes.

Some people say that budo means "the martial way" or the art of the warrior. The word *bushido* is actually closer to that meaning "the way of the warrior." Bushido is a special code of behavior and courage that samurai followed. Although budo has some of this meaning, we are interested in the more peaceful interpretation of the word.

If we look closely at the pictogram of the word (and you know what to look for), we discover that the character bu has a brush stroke that crosses out the brush stroke for spear. In much the same way, our signs with a circle and a diagonal stroke mean "no smoking, no pets, no trucks," etc. The truest meaning of budo then is, "the way of stopping the fight" or ending a conflict.

We don't want to think about martial arts as learning how to fight when we would rather respect the long history of budo; "learning how not to fight." Although a time may come when a person has to defend herself, the martial artist tries to change a situation so that the reason to fight vanishes. If we remember the *art* in martial arts, then we find that we don't want to fight at all.

Some people have suggested that we should not use the words *martial arts* but use something like *budo arts* when talking about the many schools that honor these traditions. When more people know the meaning of Do and budo, maybe we will be able to do this. What do you think?

The Samurai

The samurai were the warrior class of early Japan. Only certain people were allowed to become samurai, and it was usually an honorable occupation that was passed down in families. For a long time samurai were the only members of society who were allowed to carry swords. They had a strict code of behavior that was called *bushido*. If they broke these rules in any way, it was considered bad. This was how their society at the time was organized and a samurai placed great value in his personal honor and integrity.

The great samurai teachers were important in organizing schools where the traditions and skills were maintained as the society turned more peaceful. They helped eliminate the fighting among small groups that had upset the peace for many centuries. As the government became centered around the leadership of the Shogun, the samurai were able to promote the art of self-control and a way of learning that honored excellence. The martial arts of today are strongly affected by these traditions.

What Is the Best Martial Art?

Martial artists who have learned their history and had the chance to meet students of other schools know that this question has little meaning. It doesn't matter what style you study as long as you have a good teacher and you are a good student. If you make the effort to practice well and look for the Do in your martial art, you are on your way.

Tournament scores don't matter, numbers of students don't count, and a fancy dojo means nothing. Your effort, honesty, and what you know deep inside you is your martial art, and that is the best for you. Your teacher and your parents will help you find the best way for you to practice so that you will learn and enjoy the Way.

chapter ten

Big Ideas in the Martial Arts

Have there been times as you read this book when you've thought, "Wow, I really have to think to get this." Thinking is a great thing. Even though we all do it, we don't always do it well. Thinking is a skill that martial artists know they must practice. Like stances, it is part of what makes up your whole training.

Thinking is as an art. Philosophy is a word used for important ideas and how these ideas can be put together. People who study and teach philosophy are usually called philosophers. They write about it, talk about it, and certainly they think about it. Artists can be philosophers. Leaders in government, religion and organizations can be philosophers. Business people can be philosophers. Really anyone, including you, can become a philosopher, even if they aren't recognized or known that way.

In what ways are you affected by philosophy? Our laws are based on ideas that have come down through tradition. These ideas help us understand the thinking of the people who wrote them and the long history of thinking that has gone before. Laws and constitutions are meant to be based on the philosophies of the society that produced them.

Schools and religions have been shaped by philosophy. How we do business with each other and how we live together on our planet gives us plenty to think about. People don't always agree on their philosophies and that gives us a lot to talk about.

Martial arts schools have developed a philosophic point of view. From how martial artists live and apply what they practice, we know that philosophy is behind the traditions. Some individuals have played a big part in philosophy.

Since some of our philosophies are old, they came before books. If you think about a time before the Internet and television, imagine the effort and expense there was in sharing ideas around the world. Imagine before radio and telephone and newspapers what people had to do to communicate. Before printing was invented and ships traveled regularly—but slowly—across oceans, handwritten books and letters carried words and ideas. Before writing there was no way to record ideas except in pictures and songs where the word of one person was repeated by another and passed on. This kind of communication is called "word of mouth." We can also call it "oral tradition" because a story has to be sung or spoken to be remembered.

In chapter 9, we discussed the philosophic roots of the martial arts—how Taoism and Buddhism have played a part. Modern martial artists have been affected by Zen and Western ideas as well.

What Is Zen?

Zen is a philosophy that seems to have more questions than answers. Even though many books, poems, and essays have been written about it, most people who study Zen say that it's not about words or thinking. The most important idea from Zen that martial artists practice is being aware of this moment that we are living right now. When you are present in class, you are there not only because your body is there but because all of you is aware of your mind and spirit at the same time. You are not thinking about the past and future, but experiencing today. Zen is particularly interested in the beauty of nature and how it is always changing, such as how things are born and die. Students of Zen usually spend time meditating to clear their mind but also to open their mind to new thoughts. They are trying to understand things that are not explained by words or math.

Zen teachers often use short stories or poems to illustrate ideas for their students. They study *koan*, which are like riddles, to turn things upside down and inside out. With Zen you usually have to look at things in a completely different way to see them. The most famous Zen koan is "What is the sound of one hand clapping?" Someone once answered with the question, "If you clapped better with two hands—who would need the sound of one?" Another koan you may have heard asks, "If a tree falls in a forest, does anybody hear it?" What answer might you give to that question? What is the first thing that pops into your mind? Think about it a little and then answer it before you go to sleep. Breathe deeply and listen for the tree. Can you hear it?

Sitting on the Dock of the Bay

A good teacher was rumored to be sitting at the edge of a lake. Some students were talking about him and decided they should go see what he was doing there. After a long journey they found him.

One asked, "We see that it's beautiful by the lake. Is that why you're here?"

"No," replied the teacher.

"Are you here waiting for someone to visit you?" another asked.

"No," replied the teacher.

"Ah! Then you are here to breathe the fresh air!" a student exclaimed.

"No," replied the teacher.

The frustrated students spoke together: "Then why are you here?"

"I'm just here sitting," replied the teacher.

The students bowed to their teacher, then were invited to sit. They sat.

Understanding a Little at a Time

Like many big ideas and big apples, don't worry if you can't take it in one big bite. The big ideas in the martial arts have kept people thinking and asking questions for a long time. You may as well join in the fun of looking for answers too. Most of the pages of this book can be understood better if read more than once. As you become more advanced in your training, you can read a section again and see new things about martial arts. This is the way all good learning can be. When there is so much that you can learn, don't worry if you don't get it all. Like your stances and your kata, with practice and time it will come to you. You want to be ready to take hold and go with the flow. Take a good breath, let it out, relax, and smile. Go with kiai!

About the Authors

Claudio and Roxanne have been working together as a married couple for over ten years to create Gorindo "the Friendly Martial Art." They have co-authored books entitled *The Secret Art of Health & Fitness: Uncovered from the Martial Arts Masters and Martial Arts Mind & Body* as well as several articles and manuals for teaching martial arts. They currently reside in Bancroft, Ontario, where they are building an arts and conservation center at their retreat property near Algonquin Wilderness Park. They communicate with a global health and martial arts community through their website www.askSensei.com.

Claudio Iedwab

Claudio Iedwab is a 6th dan Black Belt in Gorindo, a 5th dan in Taekwondo, a 5th dan in Jujutsu, a 3rd dan in Karate-do, Savate French boxing and a yoga instructor. He was the 1982 South American Taekwondo Champion, the 1985 National Chinese Martial Arts Champion in Argentina, and has 25 years experience teaching young people. Claudio founded Gorindo, "The Friendly Martial Art" in 1990, integrating his studies into a non-competitive program that concentrates on health and fitness, mind and body, and the art and nature of the martial arts disciplines. In his native Argentina, Claudio was the publisher and editor of *Revista Sensei,* a martial arts magazine.

Roxanne Standefer

Roxanne Standefer is a 3rd dan Black Belt in Gorindo as well as a photographer, wilderness guide, and martial arts instructor. Before beginning her intensive studies in the martial arts, Roxanne was an education, public relations, and management consultant in outdoor recreation and the music business. As a wilderness guide and martial arts instructor, she enjoys introducing newcomers to the arts and nature she has come to love.

BOOKS OF RELATED INTEREST

TAI CHI FOR KIDS
Move with the Animals
by Stuart Alve Olson

MARTIAL ARTS TEACHING TALES
OF POWER AND PARADOX
Freeing the Mind, Focusing Chi, and Mastering the Self
by Pascal Fauliot

THE SPIRITUAL FOUNDATIONS OF AIKIDO
by William Gleason

THE THUNDERING YEARS
Rituals and Sacred Wisdom for Teens
by Julie Tallard Johnson

THE WARRIOR IS SILENT
Martial Arts and the Spiritual Path
Scott Shaw, Ph.D.

SPREAD YOUR WINGS AND FLY
An Origami Fold-and-Tell Story
by Mary Chloe Schoolcraft Saunders
Illustrated by Carla McGregor Mihelich

TWENTY JATAKA TALES
Retold by Noor Inayat Khan

Inner Traditions • Bear & Company
P.O. Box 388
Rochester, VT 05767
1-800-246-8648
www.InnerTraditions.com
Or contact your local bookseller